Margaret E. Bullock

Rock Hushka

BEST OF THE NORTHWEST

SELECTED WORKS FROM
TACOMA ART MUSEUM

TACOMA **ART** MUSEUM

Tacoma, Washington

The Northwest collection catalogue was made possible by the National Endowment for the Arts.

ART WORKS.
arts.gov

This catalogue is made possible by additional support from Edie Adams, Jeffrey and Brenda Atkin, Sandy and Laura Desner, Susan Russell Hall and Dale Hall, Lisa Hoffman and William Driscoll, Paul and Alice Kaltinick, Herb and Lucy Pruzan, The Harold & Arlene Schnitzer CARE Foundation, and the Vascovitz Family.

The texts for this publication were written by staff of Tacoma Art Museum past and present. We respectfully acknowledge the work of previous Tacoma Art Museum directors and curators.

Tacoma Art Museum
1701 Pacific Avenue
Tacoma, Washington 98402

Library of Congress Cataloging-in-Publication Data
Tacoma Art Museum.
     Best of the Northwest: selected works from Tacoma Art Museum / Margaret E. Bullock, Rock Hushka.
          pages cm
     Includes bibliographical references and index.
     ISBN 978-0-924335-36-5 (alk. paper)
     1. Painting, American—Northwestern States—Collections.
2. Painting—Washington (State)—Tacoma—Collections. 3. Tacoma Art Museum—Collections. I. Bullock, Margaret E. II. Hushka, Rock, 1966– III. Title.
ND226.T33 2012
759.197'07479788—dc23

                                        2012044180

Designed by John Hubbard
Edited by Julie Van Pelt
Proofread by Zoe Donnell and Stephanie Skrobisz
Typeset in Sonus by Maggie Lee
Printed and bound in China by Artron Color Printing Co., Ltd.

All dimensions are listed height by width by depth unless otherwise noted. Dimensions of paintings are the stretcher or support and works on paper are the image.

Cover (top to bottom; left to right):
Michael Brophy, *January* (detail), 1997. Also reproduced on page 116.
Mark Tobey, *Northwest Fantasy* (detail), 1953. Also reproduced on page 69.
Dale Chihuly, *Oxblood Soft Cylinder with Payne's Gray Drawing*, 1984. Also reproduced on page 103.
Kenjiro Nomura, *Puget Sound* (detail), circa 1933. Also reproduced on page 45.
Marie Watt, *Tear This Wall Down* (detail), 2007. Also reproduced on page 194.
Claude Zervas, *Forest #3.5* (detail), 2005. Also reproduced on page 205.
Imogen Cunningham, *On Mount Rainier 9* (detail), 1915. Also reproduced on page 33.
Mary Lee Hu, *Choker #83* (detail), 2000. Also reproduced on page 138.

Back cover: Mary Randlett, *Jacob Lawrence*, 1983. Also reproduced on page 173.
Frontispiece: Jeffrey Simmons, *Eulalia* (detail), 1998. Also reproduced on page 179.
Page 9: Dale Chihuly, *Ma Chihuly's Floats*, 1992–97. Also reproduced on page 102.
Page 11: Mark Tobey, *Northwest Fantasy*, 1953. Also reproduced on page 69.
Page 12: Ambrose Patterson, *Composition Four Figures* (detail), 1931. Also reproduced on page 35.
Page 20: Jim Hodges, *Even Here (double blue)*, 2008. Also reproduced on page 208.
Pages 30–31: Matt McCormick, *Palouse*, 2011. Chromira print, 17¼ × 27 inches (43.8 × 68.6 cm). Promised gift of Alice and Paul Kaltinick.
Page 218: Jacob Lawrence, *Street Orator's Audience*, 1936. Also reproduced on page 94.

Contents

Index of Artists

Director's Foreword and Acknowledgments

Tacoma Art Museum's story spans more than 75 years, and its history is punctuated by significant milestones. It is with great pride that we mark another important achievement and share our first major publication of highlights of the museum's Northwest art collection. Because the museum started to collect less than 50 years ago, this substantial book is a strong statement about Tacoma Art Museum's commitment to art of the Pacific Northwest and affirms the museum's leading role in scholarship and exhibitions of the highest caliber. This publication also serves as evidence that we are moving to achieve our goal of building the premier collection of Northwest art through transformative acquisitions, exhibitions, and scholarship.

Best of the Northwest: Selected Works from Tacoma Art Museum is the culmination of a series of projects and events that celebrate the museum's permanent collection and share the narrative of Northwest art. To this end the museum has also upgraded its collections management software, including eMuseum, a searchable online database of the museum's holdings. This new digital technology was made possible through the support of the Institute of Museum and Library Services, the M. J. Murdock Charitable Trust, the Driscoll Foundation, Herb and Lucy Pruzan, and Jon and Mary Shirley. Exhibition projects have focused on the museum's collection, including *A Concise History of Northwest Art* in 2009, *Collecting for the Future: The Safeco Gift and New Acquisitions* in 2011, and *Best of the Northwest: Selected Paintings from the Collection* in 2012. Begun more than three years ago, these projects have refocused the curatorial staff and brought forth rigorous new thinking about some of the most important works in the collection.

One of the museum's mandates is to spotlight the art and artists of the region. Since 1963, when the Tacoma Art League announced its name change to Tacoma Art Museum, the museum began to build a permanent collection with Northwest artists at its core. The first works to enter the collection were by such Northwest artists as Jacob Elshin, Paul Horiuchi, Beulah Hyde, and Hilda Morris. From those first acquisitions the collection has grown to more than 4,100 artworks; almost 3,000 of those works are by Northwest artists, ranging across all media and spanning from the late 19th century to the present.

We are grateful to the National Endowment for the Arts for its important support of this collection catalogue. The museum gratefully acknowledges the generous support of this publication by the following museum patrons: Edie Adams, Jeffrey and Brenda Atkin, Sandy and Laura Desner, Susan Russell Hall and Dale Hall, Lisa Hoffman and William Driscoll, Paul and Alice Kaltinick, Herb and Lucy Pruzan, The Harold & Arlene Schnitzer CARE Foundation, and the Vascovitz Family. We also want to thank the many collectors who over the years have generously donated treasured works to build the collection, the enthusiastic trustees and collection committee members who encouraged friends and family to donate works and who themselves gave,

and all those who generously provided funds to support major collection purchases. As well, we owe thanks to the museum's past directors and curators who founded and shaped the collection. And for their tremendous efforts toward creating this major publication, I personally would like to acknowledge the work of Rock Hushka, Director of Curatorial Administration and Curator of Contemporary and Northwest Art; Margaret Bullock, Curator of Collections and Special Exhibitions; and Zoe Donnell, Exhibitions and Publications Manager.

This catalogue is dedicated to the Northwest's artists for their ongoing commitment to this region, their exciting and ever-changing responses to what it means to be a Northwest artist, and their enthusiasm that has fostered a thriving, complex, and enduring art community.

Stephanie A. Stebich
Director

Curators' Acknowledgments

Traditionally, the acknowledgments sections of catalogues such as this one stress how difficult it was to choose the artists to be included, to winnow down, in this case, from more than 850 candidates to just 146 Northwest artists. Admittedly, it was a challenging and at times anxiety-ridden process—considering who to include in our summation and judging that the work in the museum's permanent collection by each artist appropriately reflected that artist's work and accomplishments. Ultimately, though, it also was a rare luxury and true pleasure to be asked to review in such depth the museum's collection of almost 3,000 works of Northwest art across all media and ranging from the late 19th century to today.

Since its founding in 1935, Tacoma Art Museum's primary focus has been the art and artists of the Northwest, and the museum's exhibition and publication histories evidence that long-standing commitment. The museum's 75th anniversary in 2010 seemed the right moment to reaffirm that mission by embarking on a major initiative to celebrate and better share the Northwest art collection through an online collection database, a series of exhibitions, and the publication of a catalogue of a stellar selection of works.

We are grateful to Stephanie Stebich, Director of Tacoma Art Museum, for wholeheartedly supporting this project. Faced with two curators proposing a major publication during an economic recession, she nevertheless enthusiastically embraced the idea, understanding the need and purpose and making it a priority. We also would like to thank Kara Hefley, Director of Development; Linda Rabadi Fair, Associate Director of Development; and Lindsey Frallic, former Manager of Foundation and Corporate Relations, for pursuing and securing a grant from the National Endowment for the Arts that provided the seed money to begin work on this publication.

Many people have been a part of making this catalogue possible, but we would like to particularly acknowledge those who have played key roles. First and foremost is Zoe Donnell, Exhibitions and Publications Manager, who handled every detail, from rounding up texts to tracking down the last little bits of needed information and managing the herculean task of keeping us on deadline. We also would like to thank Jessica Wilks, Registrar, and Ellen Ito, Exhibition and Collection Assistant, for coordinating the photography of so many works on such a short timeline; and Cyrus Smith, Preparator, for installing artworks as needed for photography. We are grateful to Alison Maurer, Curatorial Intern, for her help with many of this project's details. We also would like to thank our editor, Julie Van Pelt, for her many hours of meticulous work, and we are grateful for the collaboration of Marquand Books and their ace designer John Hubbard for a striking and thoughtful design. The individual entries in this catalogue not only reflect our work but also draw heavily from the scholarship of former museum curators, directors, and researchers. We gratefully acknowledge the research and insights they have contributed over the years and hope this catalogue honors their careful stewardship and

care of the collection. In addition to former Directors Wendell L. Ott and Chase W. Rynd, who also curated, they include the following:

Ronald G. Ahlstrom
Greg Bell
Mary Clure
Sheryl Conkelton
Barbara Johns
Jon W. Kowalek

Penelope H. Loucas
Charles M. Lovell
Jim McDonald
Patricia McDonnell
Anna C. Noll

Finally, we are grateful to the Tacoma community that has generously supported Tacoma Art Museum for more than 75 years. In return, we hope our efforts better share the museum's Northwest art collection with those who have helped to sustain it and to enhance its role, not only as a community resource, but also as a creative inspiration and regional asset.

Rock Hushka
Director of Curatorial Administration
Curator of Contemporary and Northwest Art

Margaret E. Bullock
Curator of Collections and Special Exhibitions

Margaret E. Bullock

In Hindsight
Revisiting Northwest Art before the 1960s

"The time has come," the walrus said, "to talk of many things."

—Lewis Carroll

In popular conceptions of Pacific Northwest art, and until recently reinforced by many museum presentations, the region's art history begins in the late 1940s with the artists commonly known as the Northwest Mystics: Guy Anderson (p. 62), Kenneth Callahan (p. 64), Morris Graves (p. 66), and Mark Tobey (p. 68). However, their moody, cerebral images—influenced in varying degrees by the Northwest environment, Asian aesthetics, and modernism—are the continuation rather than the start of a complex interweaving of artistic, cultural, historical, and environmental influences that characterizes the history of Northwest art.

In the last few decades, there has been steadily increasing interest in Northwest art from the 19th and first half of the 20th centuries among scholars, curators, and collectors. The history that has been uncovered is rich and multifaceted and, despite relative geographical isolation, reveals long-standing and extensive ties to the national and international art scenes. Rather than a detailed recounting, this essay surveys important influences on the art of this region before the 1960s. Tacoma Art Museum defines the Northwest broadly, based on both environmental and cultural parameters, to include Washington, Oregon, Idaho, western Montana, Alaska, and British Columbia.

A Brief Art History
The earliest artworks in the Northwest were created by the indigenous peoples of the region, who decorated their homes, clothing, everyday objects, and ceremonial regalia with a complex system of symbols and images that identified their lineage and geographical place as well as told stories. These craft traditions followed a mostly separate trajectory into the mid-20th century, distinct from other Northwest artforms. The points of intersection between these parallel histories are still to be studied.

The first non-Native artists to record the Northwest, including George Catlin and Karl Bodmer, accompanied the land survey expeditions in the late 1700s and early 1800s. As settlers moved in during the following decades, artists followed. Some, such as the well-known landscape painter Albert Bierstadt, only traveled through or stayed for brief periods. But those who settled permanently shepherded the growth of a Northwest art community by teaching classes, mentoring younger artists, forming sketch clubs where they could meet and discuss their work, and creating exhibition opportunities, notably at the numerous state and county fairs.

It was from the 1890s through the early 1900s that the art scene in the Northwest began to cohere and grow rapidly. Numerous art programs, museums, and clubs had their beginnings during this period, such as the Seattle Art School, Portland Art Museum, Tacoma Art League (precursor of Tacoma Art Museum), and the British Columbia Society of Artists. Many of these institutions, as well as state colleges and universities, offered art classes for both amateurs and professionals. Though often little known now, the artists that taught in these programs were highly trained and often actively exhibited nationally and internationally. Their skills and connections were critical in establishing a regional art community with high professional standards and global rather than provincial ambitions. Women such as Nellie Cornish, Ella Shepard Bush, and Anna B. Crocker, among others, played leading roles in this developing community as founders of art societies and institutions, working artists, teachers, curators, and collectors. It also is important to note that not only were painting and sculpture part of art programs and exhibitions but also photography, printmaking, and by the early 1900s, jewelry making.

From 1900 into the 1910s, there was a steady flow of artists to the Northwest from all parts of the United States, as well as from Europe and Asia, who brought a variety of new ideas and styles. The influx of European and European-trained artists to the Northwest and exhibitions of work by these artists sparked a noticeable change from the primarily representational images that had dominated art of the region toward more modern viewpoints. New art schools also opened during this period, including the Museum Art School at Portland Art Museum (now the Pacific Northwest College of Art), and the Oregon School of Arts and Crafts (now the Oregon College of Art and Craft), also in Portland; and Cornish School of Allied Arts (now Cornish College of the Arts) in Seattle. Their focus, and that of the older teaching institutions, increasingly shifted away from classes for the general public to the training of professional artists and a serious commitment to programs staffed by highly trained teachers and grounded in artistic theory and fundamentals. Several important exhibitions showcasing the artists of the Northwest, such as the Northwest Annuals, were also established during this decade.

The fledgling art scene in British Columbia began to flourish in the 1920s with the formation of the British Columbia Art League and the founding of the Vancouver School of Decorative and Applied Arts (now the Emily Carr University of Art and Design). Idaho's art scene became more established in the 1930s, signaled by the opening of Boise Art Museum. Schools throughout the Northwest continued to attract a mix of traditional and modernist artists, a divide that became steadily more apparent in the art press and in some exhibitions where, to avoid controversy, separate divisions and awards were offered for the two styles. Patrons and galleries were rare and the advent of the Great Depression made art a luxury for many. As part of his New Deal programs for reviving the depressed economy, President Franklin D. Roosevelt included jobs for artists to create work for government and civic buildings. The Federal Art Project programs under the Works Progress Administration were critical to the continued growth and expansion of the Northwest art scene. Not only did they offer artists a regular income, but they also encouraged a generation of Northwest artists to pursue art as a career and made art accessible to the general public, benefits that continued after the programs ended in the early 1940s.

The Federal Art Project also established rural art centers that offered exhibitions and free art classes for the public. The art centers drew progressive young artists to the Northwest as teachers who would later became important figures in the region's art community—artists such as Carl Morris (p. 162) and Guy Anderson at the Spokane Art Center and Louis Bunce (p. 72) in Salem, Oregon. The Federal Art Project was enthusiastically embraced by communities throughout the Northwest. As well, art made in the region was exhibited and installed in schools, post offices, and other government buildings all over the country, giving Northwest art greater national exposure.

Though the government art programs ended in 1942, new residents, including European war refugees, flocked to the Northwest in the 1940s and brought new ideas, energy, and opportunities. Alaska's art community saw a particular boom from this influx, reflected in the formation of the Alaska Artist Guild and inception of annual exhibitions. Postwar GI Bill benefits enabled a large number of veterans to attend college, creating a surge in enrollment in the region's art schools. Though representational images continued to be popular, art that had a social, political, moral, or spiritual message took root during the Depression years and became the preferred mode of expression for a number of Northwest artists, most notably the Northwest Mystics. National recognition of their work in the 1950s touted them as the first truly Northwest artists with a unique regional style.

The 1950s were a period of transition nationally as well as in the Northwest. The desire to forget the Depression and war years resulted in a determined rejection of tradition and embrace of the clean, spare lines of modern design, space-age architecture, and the latest inventions. On the national art scene, abstraction—particularly abstract expressionism—became the dominant style and attracted a number of practitioners in the Northwest, including William Ivey (p. 82). The 1950s also saw the beginnings of a fledgling gallery scene in major Northwest cities, dedicated to regional artists with venues such as Kharouba Gallery in Portland and the Otto Seligman Gallery in Seattle. The Northwest became the epicenter for the exploration of craft as fine art, resulting in later decades in the thriving Northwest ceramics, glass, jewelry, and fiber communities.

Looking back on this history of Northwest art prior to the 1960s, it is clear that a variety of elements were at work in shaping the subjects, styles, and even media chosen by Northwest artists. Though historical events and other factors played a role, Northwest art was primarily shaped by five critical influences: European art, American modernism, Asian aesthetics, the Northwest landscape, and a sense of community.

European Art

In the last few decades, scholars have recognized and begun to emphasize the importance of European art, both traditional and avant-garde, on the development of Northwest art. This influence stretches back to the first artists to reach the region. Since there were few art academies in America until the late 19th century, it was common for American artists to go to Europe to study, particularly to France, Germany, and Italy. Even as American art schools became more established, American-trained artists were often encouraged to give a final polish to their skills by visiting the great monuments and museums of Europe or enrolling in a well-known artist's studio for critique and further study. Many of the artists who came to the Northwest with the explorer expeditions, as well as later visitors and those who came to live, work, and teach—such as Ambrose Patterson (p. 34), Walter Isaacs (p. 54), and Peter and Margaret Camfferman (pp. 46, 47)—were European-trained and maintained their connections to the European art world throughout their careers.

The migration also occurred in reverse. The large populations that immigrated to the United States from Europe in the 19th century included many artists. Further, in the first half of the 20th century artists fled to America to escape the horrors of World War I and II. Some settled in the Northwest permanently and through their teaching and exhibiting passed on the skills and styles they had learned back home. Others, notably the modernist sculptor Alexander Archipenko and the cubist painter Amédée Ozenfant, were invited to visit and teach workshops or lecture.

It was common for the region's museums to host exhibitions of work by prominent European and American masters, often the first opportunity many Northwest artists had to see these works in person. The 1905 Lewis and Clark Centennial Exposition in Portland and the Alaska-Yukon-Pacific Exposition in Seattle in 1909 both included major art loan exhibitions, with work ranging in style from French impressionism and postimpressionism to American modernism. They offered artists and the art-loving public the chance to see historical masterworks and avant-garde works side by side and also included exhibitions of work by regional artists. The full impact of these expositions is just beginning to be understood and explored.

Because of these extensive exchanges, European styles are commonly reflected in Northwest art as in American art in general. In the early landscapes and portraits, the preference for detail and smooth finish taught in the European academies was adopted by many Northwest artists as was the grand romantic manner of painting that emphasized the drama and emotional impact of the Northwest landscape.

In the early 20th century, European influences caused a shift away from the primarily representational art that had dominated art of the region. Northwesterners found themselves face-to-face with impressionism, postimpressionism, expressionism, cubism, and surrealism. In Oregon, impressionism seems to have had the greatest impact on Northwest artists in this period, while in Washington and British Columbia the cubist and fauvist artists of the School of Paris were the dominant influences. During the 1920s expressionism and surrealism became more apparent, steadily growing in importance into the 1930s and blending with both American modernist ideas as well as regional expressions.

American Modernism

For much of the early history of American art, European and American art movements are tightly intertwined. Inspired by European artists who moved away from traditional styles to more varied possibilities, American artists also began to develop new ideas about how art could be made, how it could look, and what it could express. Though the American art academies were mostly resistant to these changes, the Art Students League in New York, in addition to artist-run schools and clubs, became the primary training ground for nontraditional artists. Many Northwest artists—including sculptor Hilda Morris (p. 164), painter Z. Vanessa Helder (p. 56), printmaker and illustrator Thomas Handforth (p. 52), and jeweler Margaret De Patta (p. 58)—trained at the Art Students League or other avant-garde schools. Through their subsequent roles as teachers or working artists, they brought to the Northwest forward-looking ideas, including the importance of everyday people and events as subjects, expressive rather than descriptive use of color, manipulated space, reduction of form, and art as a vehicle for social or personal commentary.

As with European art, museum exhibitions and the art exhibitions at the 1905 and 1909 expositions also were important opportunities for Northwest artists to see work by both traditional and modernist American artists, notably the impressionists and the members of the social realist group known as The Eight, or Ashcan School.

By the 1930s, elements of modernism were present in most Northwest art, though it took many forms and was adopted in varying degrees, from the expressive color used by Peggy Strong (p. 49), to the flattened space and reductive detail found in Kenjiro Nomura's work (p. 45), to the European-inflected experiments of Spencer Moseley (p. 145). Art that had a social, political, moral, or spiritual message became common. American regionalism also was a dominant influence. Countrywide, there was growing interest in American Scene painting—depictions of everyday life in America—and in describing regional identities and art forms. This interest was further encouraged under the government's Federal Art Project. Imagery about a region's history or working people was preferred for government buildings and though not required in other instances was the most common. The Northwest's pioneer and logging histories also were popular subjects, but the region's unique natural environment was considered its defining characteristic and was quickly adopted by critics and curators inside and outside the region as the primary way to recognize and explain Northwest art. Though this tendency often lumped together works in very disparate styles and ignored other key influences, it has proved to be powerful and long-lived and still continues to direct discussions of the region's art today.

By the 1950s, with Europe still struggling to recover from the devastations of World War II and many of its leading artists recent immigrants to the United States, New York became the new center for the international avant-garde, most notably the abstract expressionist movement. An important West Coast arm of this movement centered in the California School of Fine Arts (now the San Francisco Art Institute). A number of Northwest artists rapidly adopted this new style, with its focus on the process and materials of art making and an artist's individual vision rather than subject matter. Artists such as Frank Okada (p. 163) also experimented with other related forms of pure abstraction such as color field painting, paralleling in the Northwest what was happening in the larger American art world.

Asia

The influence of Asian aesthetics on Northwest art was early and extensive. During the 19th century, increased contact with Japan and China led to a craze in Europe and America for artworks and decorative objects in the styles of these countries. This trend was particularly evident in interior decoration and in objects such as furniture and porcelain, which were common in the Northwest because of its close trading ties with Asia and large Asian immigrant populations. In art, the impressionists and postimpressionists adopted both the technique and look of Japanese woodblock prints. Northwest printmakers, including brothers Waldo and W. Corwin Chase, created woodblock prints of Northwest scenes that clearly drew from Japanese compositions. Other artists were attracted to the compressed space, strong diagonals, and dynamic viewpoints common to these images and to Chinese painting. Communities of Asian and Asian American artists gathered in the Northwest's larger cities, supporting and encouraging each other's work but also becoming integrally involved in the broader Northwest art community as both friends and artistic collaborators. As well, a number of Northwest artists—notably Guy Anderson, Kenneth Callahan, Morris Graves, and Mark Tobey—were fascinated by the philosophies and cultures of Asia, traveling there, collecting art objects, and adopting Buddhist and Taoist philosophies.

Asian aesthetics were particularly pivotal in the growth and look of Northwest photography. In the 1890s the most popular style of photography both nationally and in the Northwest was pictorialism, a movement committed to exploring and promoting the artistic potential of photography by creating manipulated, painterly images. The subjects and compositions of these works often were drawn from Asian art, and by the 1920s many of the photographers were themselves immigrants to the Northwest from Japan and China. In Seattle, Kyo Koike (p. 40), Frank Asakichi Kunishige (p. 41), and Yukio Morinaga (p. 38), along with other photographers, founded the Seattle Camera Club, a short-lived but highly influential organization. Such photographers' images of the Northwest landscape in particular are reminiscent of Asian landscape paintings and affected how other artists chose to depict the mountains, fog, and waters of the Northwest.

The Landscape

The extent of the Northwest landscape's impact on Northwest art has been much written about and debated. Visually dramatic, persistently lush, endlessly mutable, and always inescapably present, even in the region's cities, this landscape shapes every visitor's and resident's physical and visual experience. As part of the broader West, the Northwest landscape also is freighted with beliefs about what it means to travel or live here. Independent, nonconformist, hardy, outdoorsy: these are all terms that have been associated with regional identity since the western territories became part of the nation, and they are deeply embedded characteristics of the region's self-definition today. Whether consciously or unconsciously, these factors have certainly influenced artistic interpretations of the Northwest, but the extent has varied by artist, interest, and time period.

The work of the artists who accompanied the explorer expeditions in the late 1700s and early 1800s, such as that of Paul Kane, was primarily documentary, but their evocative images of the frontier Northwest's peoples and environments inspired other adventurers, and eventually settlers, to travel west to see for themselves. For the many landscape painters who visited or settled in the region later in the 19th century—including Thomas Hill, Robert Swain Gifford, and James Everett Stuart—the landscapes of the West fulfilled America's desire to claim for the young nation ancient and God-given roots. Their images also recorded and celebrated these new and seemingly endless resources for achieving the nation's driving ambitions. Their compositions drew either from the European romantic landscape tradition, designed to overwhelm viewers with the grandeur of what they were seeing, or from European and American schools of picturesque landscape painting that strove for balanced, carefully composed "views" in which landscape elements were often reworked or rearranged to achieve the desired effect. Though many of the resulting pictures were less than accurate, they still captured the great beauty and physical impact of the Northwest landscape.

For the photographers and impressionist painters, the Northwest's abundant open spaces, varied landscapes, and constantly shifting light effects were an endless source of inspiration and tailor-made to suit their interests, as evident in the work of painters John Davidson Butler and C. C. McKim and photographers such as Myra Wiggins (p. 39). For those who worked with modern ideas about spatial construction, color, and mood, and rejected long-standing artistic traditions, the Northwest landscape was sometimes muse and sometimes of no interest. The responses are as varied as the artists, even in the 1930s, when the regionalist movement codified the landscape as the Northwest's defining characteristic. Some artists, such as Kenneth Callahan or Carl Hall (p. 57), continued to choose landscape as a subject but compressed space, reduced forms, focused on color contrasts, and used other modernist variations in their depictions. Others seemed to find the landscape incidental, focusing on portraits, interiors, city scenes, or still lifes and using palettes based on new color theories rather than on the artists' surroundings. And for some, notably Morris Graves, the mystique of the Northwest landscape—its moody omnipresence and sometimes primeval atmosphere—was integral to the look and feel of their work even when it was not specifically about the landscape. In the work of the abstractionists of the 1940s and 1950s, it is more difficult to trace the influence the environment may have had, but the work of many artists shows a noticeable interest in a more muted, organic palette, and inherent in numerous works is the diffused, subtle Northwest light that illuminated these artists' studios.

Northwest Native Cultures

The influence of Northwest Native cultures and artists on Northwest art prior to the 1960s has not been explored in depth. In historical works there are some direct borrowings of symbols and imagery and depictions of Native objects such as masks and totem poles. A handful of Native artists who chose to work within the Anglo art community, such as Julius Twohy (p. 51), have been identified though not fully researched. Certainly the bold, stylized imagery common to Northwest Native art would have interested the modernists who were experimenting with these ideas in their own work. In addition, under the auspices of the Federal Art Project's Index of American Design in the 1930s many Northwest Native craft objects were recorded indicating a sincere appreciation for these works, but individual artists were rarely named.

The displacement and denigration of Native groups during the settling and growth of the western states is well documented and explains the lack of apparent ties between the Northwest's Anglo and Native artists. However, further work is needed to explore how Native arts were viewed by Northwest artists and the role they played in the development of Northwest art.

Community

The tenacious desire to create and maintain an arts community in the Northwest was critical to its growth and survival. From the earliest days, artists created opportunities to train others, exhibit their work, and educate the public. Numerous clubs and societies formed over the decades, offering lectures and providing forums for the exchange of information and ideas, as well as opportunities for artists to make and discuss their work with their peers. These arts organizations also held exhibitions that were rare public venues for showing and selling work. Artists advocated for and helped found art schools and museums as well as regular and more prominent regional exhibitions. The interconnectedness of the visual arts with regional dance, music, literature, and theater is just beginning to be explored but also appears to have been significant in the development of Northwest art in myriad ways, ranging from reciprocal inspiration to shared resources to mutual support.

Critical as well was the art community's determination to be part of the larger national and international art scenes, whether through training, exhibition, or collegial networks. These connections were critical in signaling the region's artistic ambitions as well as insuring the community's continued access to work and ideas from outside the Northwest. Collectors also played a role by bringing European and American works to the Northwest and lending them out for exhibition so that Northwest artists could see them firsthand. Many such patrons ultimately gave their collections to help found or enhance newly fledged museums.

Histories become more intriguing with greater hindsight. The Northwest's earlier art history has gained new prominence as its breadth and complexity has become increasingly evident. A number of regional museums now regularly collect, exhibit, and publish on work from this period. Historical Northwest art is now an acceptable subject for graduate theses and dissertations. A small but enthusiastic group of collectors have created a demand for historical Northwest art, which has encouraged still further sleuthing for forgotten bodies of work and lesser-known artists.

Exciting new work is just beginning to be presented and written about, on such diverse topics as Asian and Asian American artists in the Northwest, gay and lesbian artists, and histories of organizations that played pivotal roles. In-depth studies of issues touched upon in this essay, such as the influence of particular avant-garde styles on Northwest artists, are becoming more common. That there are so many new topics still to be explored is the best proof of the region's diverse and complex art history and the best argument for never forgetting to periodically pause and look back.

SELECTED SOURCES CONSULTED AND RECOMMENDED READING

Ament, Deloris Tarzan. *Iridescent Light: The Emergence of Northwest Art*. La Conner: Museum of Northwest Art in association with University of Washington Press, 2002.

Cleaver, J. D. "Introduction to Oregon Art History." In *Oregon Painters: The First Hundred Years (1859–1959),* ed. Ginny Allen and Jody Klevit, 1–26. Portland: Oregon Historical Society Press, 1999.

Conkelton, Sheryl. *What It Meant to be Modern: Seattle Art at Mid-Century*. Seattle: Henry Gallery Association, University of Washington, 2000.

Conkelton, Sheryl, and Laura Landau. *Northwest Mythologies: The Interactions of Mark Tobey, Morris Graves, Kenneth Callahan, and Guy Anderson*. Tacoma: Tacoma Art Museum in association with University of Washington Press, 2003.

Griffin, Rachael, "Portland and Its Environs." In *Art of the Pacific Northwest: From the 1930s to the Present,* 3–38. Washington, DC: National Collection of Fine Arts, Smithsonian Institution Press, 1974.

Harrington, LaMar. *Ceramics in the Pacific Northwest: A History*. Index of Art in the Pacific Northwest no. 10. Seattle: Henry Art Gallery, University of Washington Press, 1979.

Harthorn, Sandy, and Kathleen Bettis. *One Hundred Years of Idaho Art, 1850–1950*. Boise: Boise Art Museum, 1990.

Hull, Roger. "The Lure of Pacific Northwest Art." *American Art Review* 11, no. 1 (1999): 168–77.

Impert, John. "Hidden in Plain Sight: Northwest Impressionism, 1910–1935." PhD dissertation, University of Washington, Seattle, 2012.

Johns, Barbara, ed. *Jet Dreams: Art of the Fifties in the Northwest*. Seattle: Tacoma Art Museum in association with University of Washington Press, 1995.

Kangas, Matthew. *Epicenter: Essays on North American Art*. Seattle: Midmarch Arts Press, 2004.

Kingsbury, Martha. *Art of the Thirties: The Pacific Northwest*. Seattle: University of Washington Press, 1972.

———. "Seattle and the Puget Sound." In *Art of the Pacific Northwest: From the 1930s to the Present,* 39–92. Washington, DC: National Collection of Fine Arts, Smithsonian Institution Press, 1974.

———. *Celebrating Washington's Art: An Essay on 100 Years of Art in Washington*. Olympia: 1989 Washington Centennial Commission, 1989.

Kreisman, Lawrence, and Glenn Mason. *The Arts and Crafts Movement in the Pacific Northwest*. Portland: Timber Press, 2007.

Martin, David F. *An Enduring Legacy: Women Painters of Washington, 1930–2005*. Seattle: Whatcom Museum of History and Art in association with University of Washington Press, 2005.

Martin, David F., and Nicolette Bromberg. *Shadows of a Fleeting World: Pictorial Photography and the Seattle Camera Club*. Seattle: University of Washington Press, 2011.

Murray, Joan. *Canadian Art in the Twentieth Century*. Toronto: Dundurn Press, 1999.

Raban, Jonathan. Introduction to *The Pacific Northwest Landscape: A Painted History,* ed. Kitty Harmon, 7–94. Seattle: Sasquatch, 2000.

Reid, Dennis. *A Concise History of Canadian Painting*: Toronto: Oxford University Press Canada, 1988.

Woodward, Kesler. *Painting in the North: Alaskan Art in the Anchorage Museum of History and Art*. Seattle: University of Washington Press, 1993.

Rock Hushka

Dissolving the Notion of Northwest Style to Articulate Northwest Identity

The quest to identify regional identity in contemporary art is fraught with complexity and contradiction. At the most basic level, artists generally resist a geographical qualifier because by definition it places their work outside a broader context. Most artists would insist that their work and interests result from larger and more vital issues than a singular obsession with regional concerns. Curators and arts writers, on the other hand, have a more vested interest in the idea of place. Curators find themselves delving into questions of regional identity because their institutions seek to preserve and celebrate accomplishments of the artists who live within a certain area. Part of this imperative derives from placing the artists who live and work in the region at the center of a society that values creativity and achievement. Art produced in the region codifies the aspirations, abilities, and interests that inform our daily lives. Tacoma Art Museum's collections represent the strength, pluck, and vision that we share as the Pacific Northwest.

The history of contemporary Northwest art almost always begins with reflection upon the legacy of the art exhibitions assembled for the 1962 Century 21 Exposition, more commonly known as the Seattle World's Fair. The fair's exhibitions were important because regional artists were comprehensively presented to a national audience for the first time. Additionally, and perhaps more importantly, the artists and their supporters were able to view the broader national and international context in which they were working.

Visitors to the fair had a rare opportunity to compare the strengths, accomplishments, and interests of the region's artists with those of internationally acclaimed artists. On one level, the exhibitions shared certain features. There was heavy emphasis on gestural abstraction, with a small number of figural works and hard-edged geometric abstractions. Landscape was minimally represented. On another level, the Northwest works appeared slightly out of step and lacked a breadth of scope and eagerness to embrace the newest ideas.

One of the unintended consequences of the fair was that a sense of inferiority coalesced around the work produced by regional artists. An ethos began to emerge that in the absence of significant recognition from a major art center (usually New York, but occasionally London and Paris), an artist's career was considered restricted to a modest level of success. The Seattle World's Fair focused attention on the shortcomings of the region's artistic production, challenging regional artists to reach the level of refinement, conceptual strength, and virtuosity found in the fair's two *Art since 1950* exhibitions of contemporary art.

The international section of *Art since 1950* featured works by artists such as Francis Bacon, Henry Moore, Pierre Soulages, Rufino Tamayo, and Jean Tinguely. The national selection included works by Lee Bontecou, Helen Frankenthaler, Jasper Johns, Ellsworth Kelly, Joan Mitchell, Isamu Noguchi, Georgia O'Keeffe, and Jackson Pollock, among many others. In the national section, the Northwest was represented only by Morris Graves (p. 66), Paul Horiuchi (p. 70), and Mark Tobey (p. 68) as well as Washington native Robert Motherwell (p. 92).

The region's contemporary artists were showcased in *Northwest Art Today* and a survey of works by Mark Tobey from Seattle Art Museum's permanent collection. Tobey's one-person exhibition was significant because he was the Northwest's most distinguished and critically acclaimed artist; he had prominent representation in New York's Willard Gallery and was widely celebrated as an important influence on Jackson Pollock, who credited Tobey's "white writing" with the development of his overall compositional style.

These exhibitions gave the impression that quality and a distinguished artistic identity were linked more closely to art production in New York and London than to a cohesive regional style. Concluding his introduction to the *Northwest Art Today* catalogue, Millard B. Rogers, the exhibition's director, conceded, "Perhaps in these paintings and sculpture some will see a common spirit, or distinctive features, that may justify the term 'Northwest Art.' On the other hand one may view these works as but one fact of a truly international style that embraces all of Twentieth Century art, which tends to be non-figurative, highly emotional, and even violent."[1]

Reflecting on the works included in *Northwest Art Today,* it is clear that, already in 1962, the Northwest's most active artists were looking to ideas beyond regional concerns to inform their artistic explorations. Artists sought to develop personal styles founded in an individualism that supported abstract expressionism and, by extension, the freedom to move beyond a painterly abstraction and into op art and collage.

In retrospect, this freedom and imperative to explore personal styles discernibly rejected the idea of a "Northwest school." Composed of Guy Anderson, Kenneth Callahan, Morris Graves, and Mark Tobey, the Northwest school was declared by *Life* magazine's 1953 feature "Mystic Painters of the Northwest."[2] The uncited author remarked that the mist and rain, the forests, and the region's proximity to East Asia were paramount features of the region's art.[3]

The stylistic hallmarks of the Northwest school—such as an overt spiritual content, appropriation of Asian imagery and symbolism, muted colors, and the thin, smooth application of paints—were clearly considered out of fashion by many of the artists featured in *Northwest Art Today.* Although their styles may have seemed passé, Tobey, and to a lesser extent Graves, Callahan, and Anderson, remained the touchstones for success. Their collectors, their museum exhibitions, and their dominance within the region's art criticism marked a distinct divergence between the generations.

This drift away from precedent and the influence of Tobey signaled that Northwest artists were voraciously interested in the "new" or the "avant-garde" rather than in continuing the lines of thought and interest of the "master." Primarily, this might be understood as the artists' generational search to define their own era on their terms. In the 1960s, this manifested as intriguing explorations of second-generation abstract expressionism, op art, and new approaches to figuration. This would soon be followed by experiments in color field painting, minimalism, and pop.

There are fascinating examples of efforts to move beyond the "Northwest Masters" even before the 1962 world's fair. A singular highlight is the early abstraction *Nostalgia #2* by Chuck Close (p. 120), a student effort to paint in the manner of Willem de Kooning. The painting was the first exhibited by the artist in the Northwest Annual at Seattle Art Museum in 1960.

After he left the Northwest, Close quickly shed his expressionist efforts and began to explore the possibilities of photorealism. The arc of Close's career offers an interesting example of how Northwest artists develop certain stages of their career in the area and then seek to fulfill their ambitions by moving to the East. Close's success has its foundation in his early training and experiences in the Northwest, but his development and critical acclaim stems entirely from his work outside the region. Generations of artists followed this career trajectory. Born in Monroe, Washington, and having spent a good portion of his childhood in Tacoma, Close has become one of the most respected painters of his generation, exhibiting in major museums around the world, such as his 1998 retrospective organized by the Museum of Modern Art, New York. After a serious medical crisis left him with limited mobility (Close refers to this as "the incident"), the artist had to relearn motor control in his arms and his style changed to accommodate his challenges with dexterity. *Lucas,* a portrait of his colleague Lucas Samaras, is an excellent example of his later work (p. 121).

Interestingly, this rejection of a distinct regionalism may also have roots in the ideological battles of the Cold War. Art historian Serge Guilbaut outlines the effect of such political pressures as Americans sought dominance over the Soviet Union after World War II. Guilbaut details the gambits levied through art and criticism for the covert promotion of the class of abstract expressionists.[4]

With this radical new abstraction, markets as well as covert government agencies discovered a new tool to promote the vigorous character of the United States and defend the values of liberty and freedom against Soviet communism, which American artist communities were perceived as embracing and promoting. The ascendancy of abstraction dealt a catastrophic blow to artists who created images typical of regional art, such as landscapes and figurative work depicting the dignity of the working class. Such images were critiqued as old-fashioned or, worst of all, kitsch. Given the unexpected injection of the "space race" into the gestalt of the 1962 world's fair, the headlong rush into the modern by regional artists should not be underestimated.

As he sought to articulate a clear theme for *Northwest Art Today,* Millard Rogers noted, "The implication is that in the extreme Northwest corner of the United States there are conditions, the isolation of this section of the country, its soft light, dark forests, mist, and rain, that have led to a distinctly different type of American art."[5] Yet, the evidence of a different and distinct art was modest at best. Seeds planted during the 1960s established a vigorous art community that sought to define itself in terms and ambitions that reached beyond the earlier generation's regionalist affinities.

Rogers's conditional statement articulated the polarity between an affinity to regional identity and the desire and eagerness to engage in the most recent ideas and themes in contemporary art. Therein lies the fundamental crisis in artistic identity: because regional artists are so far removed from the art centers, there is little optimism that regional voices and images will be valued outside their geographic area. Art critics have discussed this conundrum every decade since the world's fair, and this tension in new forms continues to inform efforts to make sense of a Northwest artistic identity.

In 1968, the art critics Peter Selz and Tom Robbins collaborated on a pair of articles that offered an overview of the state of the region's art.[6] Both critics rewarded the absence of discernibly regional imagery and concerns. Selz commented with some degree of astonishment, "I was impressed by the high quality of some of the works (much of it coming from the town of Ellensburg, Washington) and the absence of any vestige of regionalism."[7] Robbins concluded with conviction, "The best contemporary Northwest artists have jettisoned geographical ties in order to interlock freely with those international forces most crucial in the mainstream of art."[8]

Again in 1970, Robbins emphatically railed against engagement with overtly regional concerns:

Let us hurry to seize the term "Northwest art," nail it in a Haida coffin, weight it down with a ton of bronze bird sculptures and sink it in the deepest part of Puget Sound, marking the spot with a buoy decorated by quasi-Chinese calligraphers in order that innocent sailboats and carefree yellow submarines might keep their distance.

There was a time when "Northwest art" signified a regional school of low-keyed painting that dealt with nature in a more or less mystical fashion. That application has not been relevant in years. The art produced in this region today reflects a multitude of philosophies and styles. The better artists locally are dealing with the problems and impulses that concern better artists everywhere. The designation "Northwest art" has always been provincial. Now, it is a lie as well.[9]

In retrospect, Robbins's dismissal of regional identity is fascinating. He obviously sought to push the local arts community to a higher level of ambition and achievement through a more rigorous art practice and his informed commentary. But his indictment of a generalized, local malaise may be questioned as too strong a statement against the impulse to celebrate the region. Despite his interest in moving toward only "cutting edge" art, the effects of sharing a regional geography, cultural experience, and societal structure simply cannot be ignored. When he was writing, the Northwest economy was struggling as Boeing began to contract in one of its deeper cyclical declines. The region still smarts with the memory of the infamous billboard, "Will the last person leaving Seattle—turn out the lights."[10]

Economic recession notwithstanding, Jacob Lawrence's (p. 94) arrival at the University of Washington boosted the arts community in 1970. A paragon in American art, with roots in the Harlem Renaissance of the late 1930s, Lawrence inspired a reinvigorated interest in figuration and narrative imagery. He also brought with him a profound and abiding love of place as a critical subject for painting.[11] Lawrence was a towering presence and an enormously influential teacher for decades, mentoring artists such as Barbara Earl Thomas (p. 75). He also opened a vital critical space for other figurative artists such as Fay Jones (p. 129) and Jay Backstrand (p. 98).

The extent of the radical departure from the somber, internal worlds of Mark Tobey and Morris Graves may also be found in Alden Mason's *Burpee* series of the early 1970s (p. 152). Based on childhood memories of the ubiquitous seed catalogues, the series captured the colors, promise, and excitement that followed the catalogues' arrival. The brilliant colors and large scale of these works finally shattered the expectation of regional abstraction in the tradition of Tobey,

Graves, and their followers. Mason's application of vibrant, thinned pigments bridged the impulse toward individualism as idealized by the abstract expressionists and the newer ideals of the color field painters. Mason's *Burpee* paintings stand as a milestone in the redirection of Northwest art.

The 1970s also marked a distinctly different and energized presentation of contemporary art. The Northwest led the nation in government funding for public art projects, as exemplified by 1% for Art, established in King County in 1973. State programs in Washington and Oregon followed soon after. Additionally, the multidisciplinary and/or gallery (lowercased in the vernacular of the day) was founded in 1974 in part to foster experimentation in electronic art and music. By the end of the decade, artists were working to create the Center on Contemporary Art (CoCA), which opened for its first exhibitions in 1980. These institutions set the bar for integrating the most forward-thinking art on the national level with the most promising new work by local artists.

The performance artist Dennis Evans came to national attention during the mid-1970s. His ritual performances and objects (p. 96) garnered critical acclaim. Selected for the 1978 Whitney Biennial, Evans was even featured by the mainstream *Newsweek* for his elaborate performances that incorporated traditional religious symbolism and rituals. Evans would continue to seek inspiration across disciplines, twining the hard sciences (astronomy, physics, geology, etc.) with the complex thinking of social sciences (linguistics, theology, philosophy). Evans and his cohort—mainly the artists affiliated with the Linda Farris Gallery—blazed new territory and established national critical reputations.

Summarizing this energy in 1986, arts writer Bill Berkson noted in *Art in America*,

> Serious art in Seattle seems to have come by its peculiar brand of cosmopolitanism in successive waves, none of them conclusive, none in fact very cumulative. Glimmers of modernism appeared in the paintings of Ambrose Patterson (Derain, Matisse) by the 1920s and of Walter Isaacs (Matisse, Cézanne, Braque) by the '30s. . . . What Tom Robbins called in 1968 "a curious spectrum of provincialism and hip" has been transmuted to what a critic of the '80s, given the present grab bag of classifications, could label "regional pluralism"— i.e., the same plethora of styles as elsewhere but with markedly regional twists and limitations.[12]

One of the illustrations for a second Berkson article was *Dying Light in Venice* by Randy Hayes (p. 126).[13]

Unfortunately, Berkson limited his attention to artists working in Seattle and, while providing important descriptions of individual artists, neglected to articulate those "markedly regional twists and limitations." He did leave important clues. He lavishly praised the vibrancy of the public art program. He noted the strength of the artist community. And he acknowledged the wide range of stylistic approaches embraced by the city's artists.

One of the milestones for the arts community in the 1980s was the exhibition *Outside New York: Seattle* at the New Museum in New York and later at Seattle Art Museum. The New Museum's curator, Ned Rifkin, selected eight artists to represent the city, including Paul Berger (p. 106), Marsha Burns (p. 107), Dennis Evans, Randy Hayes, and Fay Jones. This exhibition presented the most advanced art from the Northwest in the very center of the art world, and Rifkin deliberately sidestepped the issue of regionalism: "This exhibition has not been thematically derived. Nor does it purport to address or define the rather significant issue of a regional sensibility endemic to Seattle. . . . However, I have deliberately chosen to present these eight artists in terms of the individual achievement and commitment embodied in their work."[14] For Rifkin and other curators, critics, and collectors, the emphasis was on individual excellence, with the knowledge that regionalism was a powerful undercurrent.

Publications and arts writing in the Northwest became demonstrably stronger. Critics at both daily and alternative newspapers in Seattle and Portland provided important viewpoints about new works and exhibitions. One of the key publications from the decade was Bruce Guenther's *50 Northwest Artists*.[15] With its portraits by Marsha Burns, this book remains an indispensable resource on the history of Northwest art.

By the 1980s, the Northwest had also solidified its reputation as a national leader for artwork with roots in the traditional crafts. Indicative of this energy was the flourishing of the Pilchuck Glass School. Founded in 1971 by Dale Chihuly and art patrons Anne Gould Hauberg and John H. Hauberg, Pilchuck became a world leader in glass experimentation and teaching.[16] Chihuly decided to return to the Northwest full-time in 1983, thereby ensuring the sustained prominence of the school and the art world's attention on the region.[17]

The importance of craft-based media is critical to understanding the development of Northwest art and the growing sense of an artist community. This required decades of work and cooperation by artists, institutions, and schools. Pilchuck notwithstanding, the genesis was the GI bill, which made training in art and crafts accessible for a generation of soldiers after World War II.[18] Institutions such as Bellevue Art Museum (now Bellevue Arts Museum) and its annual Art Fair and the numerous guilds, such as the Seattle Metals Guild, provided commercial and exhibition opportunities for artists.

Additionally, schools such as Central Washington University and its metals program, with its distinguished instructors such as Ken Cory (p. 80); the University of Washington's metals, ceramic, and fiber programs; and the Oregon College of Art and Craft all contributed to building a strong and renowned craft tradition.

The critical contributions of this approach in the 1980s dissolved boundaries between traditional crafts and fine arts. Artists such as Dale Chihuly (p. 102), Layne Goldsmith (p. 195), Mary Lee Hu (p. 138), Howard Kottler (p. 78), Nancy Mee (p. 156), and Nancy Worden (p. 198) wholly and purposely blurred the distinction between craft and art. These artists' works and careers demonstrate that technique, intent, and critical content meld regardless of form. These artists helped establish a system that encouraged the blending and mixing of process and media and set the stage for resurgent engagement through materials by artists such as Leo Saul Berk (p. 204), Claire Cowie (p. 128), and Jeffry Mitchell (p. 160).

Institutionally, the Museum of Northwest Art in La Conner relocated and expanded in 1991, an important signal of increasing interest in the regional scene. Local writers, including Patricia Failing and Ron Glowen, in their articles for both local and national arts publications, sought to describe a general sense of anxiety about the strength of regional art. This anxiety was reflected in the popularity of grunge music, with the nervous chords of "Smells Like Teen Spirit" wafting from radios across the country.

Glowen frankly wrote, "The visual art scene is listless."[19] Failing quoted Jo-Anne Birnie Danzker, former director of the Vancouver Art Gallery and current director of Frye Art Museum in Seattle, describing the Vancouver art situation: "Canada is in the process of going through something like a cultural revolution. We're not only confronting problems with Quebec, but also the land claims of the aboriginal people, women's rights, and the civil rights of many different ethnic communities. We're sitting on a tinderbox, and it's not surprising to find that artists are sensitive to these concerns."[20] Failing also described a backlash against public art by some in the artist community. She quoted artist Charles Krafft, "who recently lambasted the 'shameless spawn of grant-sucking lampreys who have made an aptitude for freeloading on public funds the sine qua non of career legitimacy in Seattle.'"[21] As for Portland, Failing reported that "few knowledgeable observers would argue that the visual arts are taking off in Portland," and she more direly cited a report by the National Arts Stabilization Fund: "striking fact—while there is a broad general support for the arts in Portland, there are few individuals . . . for whom the arts are a burning passion."[22]

Conversely, local identity was boosted by the explosive growth of corporations such as Amazon.com, Costco, Microsoft, Nike, and Starbucks. Perhaps in an effort to solidify achievements, and stemming from an observable need to support the visual arts, a variety of projects emerged to assess the progress and strengths of the region's art and artists. The Oregon Biennial at Portland Art Museum was infused with a new energy and sense of purpose in 1997, and the Northwest Biennial at Tacoma Art Museum began in 1991. Bellevue Art Museum reinvigorated the Northwest Annual exhibitions. Additionally, Tacoma Art Museum initiated its 12th Street Series (now the Northwest Perspective Series), an annual one-person exhibition exploring in depth a midcareer artist's development. Lastly, the Behnke Foundation established the Neddy Artist Fellowship, providing an additional, independent award for artistic excellence.

By the end of the decade, regional artists found their voice, partly through an embrace of the regional. Leo Saul Berk, Michael Brophy (p. 116), Mark Takamichi Miller (p. 158), and Susan Seubert (p. 196) embodied this profound shift. These artists seemed to defy the naysaying critics and began to express aesthetic visions that meshed regional identifiers with solid conceptual foundations. The era marked a return to a pride of place.

Institutionally, the same sense of confidence began to manifest in major building projects after 2000. Bellevue Arts Museum, Portland Art Museum, Seattle Art Museum, the Northwest Museum of Arts and Culture in Spokane, the Museum of Contemporary Craft in Portland, the Whatcom Museum of History and Art (now the Whatcom Museum) in Bellingham, the Jordan Schnitzer Museum of Art at the University of Oregon in Eugene, the Hallie Ford Museum of Art at Willamette University in Salem, and Tacoma Art Museum completed major new building projects.[23]

This explosive growth was mirrored by the activity in commercial galleries in Vancouver (British Columbia), Portland, Seattle, and Tacoma. Some of these galleries participated in international art fairs in Miami, Chicago, New York, Los Angeles, and London, showcasing the ambition and talent of the region's artists. Responding to this trend, Seattle artists Jaq Chartier and Dirk Park established Aqua Art Miami in 2005. In Portland, the short-lived Affair at the Jupiter Hotel offered a heady mix of regional galleries from across the United States.

Additionally, curators at all the local museums began to examine the work of local artists in an energized way. Importantly, both Portland Art Museum and Tacoma Art Museum established positions for a curator of Northwest art. Lisa Corrin at Seattle Art Museum and Elizabeth Brown at the

Henry Art Gallery assessed the state of regional art for the magazine *Modern Painters:*

> This prevailing sense of possibility and evolving identity is so Seattle. The weather appears relentlessly grim, but then the fog lifts and one sees in every direction the endless… peaks of the Olympics to the west, Cascades to the east, Mt. Baker to the north, and to the south, the imperious Mt. Rainier. When the Seattle art community says, 'the mountain is out,' it is staring at a cliché as well as the reality—the challenging peak it must scale to both stake its claim and get a panoramic view of what lies beyond the northwest region.[24]

Brown and Corrin also noted that "some of Seattle's most accomplished and celebrated artists have chosen to move elsewhere. They include: minimalist painter Jo Baer, Spokane-born Jim Hodges, former museum security guard Charles LeDray,… painter Cameron Martin, conceptual glass artist Josiah McElheny, LA-bound sculptor Patrick Holderfield,… and photographer Robert Lyons."[25] This list should also have named the distinguished artists who drew inspiration from the region and established thriving studios there. By 2010, in Seattle and Vancouver, British Columbia, this included such internationally renowned artists as Janet Cardiff and George Bures Miller, Dale Chihuly, Rodney Graham, Gary Hill, Ken Lum, Roy McMakin, Jock Sturges, Trimpin, and Jeff Wall. In Portland, Harrell Fletcher, Arnold J. Kemp (p. 155), and Gus Van Sant established studios. And Robert Adams, Anne Appleby (p. 184), John Buck (p. 104), Deborah Butterfield, Chuck Close, Ed and Nancy Kienholz, Agnes Martin, Robert Motherwell, and Jessica Stockholder have Northwest connections or roots.[26]

These artists' success can be attributed to a multiplicity of factors. First, institutional and commercial support has been broad and sustained. Artists increasingly find their works in local museum collections and publications that support their artistic visions. Commercial success outside the region, along with growing local support, has enabled these artists to remain settled in the area. Lastly, the Internet and other forms of instantaneous communication have seemingly shortened the distance between the Northwest and the more powerful art centers.

In 2003 a broad survey organized by seven curators, *Baja to Vancouver: The West Coast and Contemporary Art,* provocatively examined the current state of art along the western edge of the continent and provided insights into the region's multiplicity of styles and interests.[27] Responding to the project, a group of artists and curators in Portland, led by Randy Gragg and Matthew Stadler, organized *Core Sample: Portland Art Now,* a citywide series of events and exhibitions in October 2003.[28] *Core Sample* highlighted regional artists' diversity of approaches and themes but focused almost exclusively on Oregon artists. Interestingly, the exhibition *LAVA 2002* predated *Core Sample* and focused on artists associated with one studio building in Seattle.[29]

Perhaps most visibly, Tacoma Art Museum increased its commitment to regional artists by honing its collecting focus to the Pacific Northwest, bolstering the Northwest Perspective Series to include a major publication and reinvigorating the Northwest Biennial to include a more rigorous curatorial focus and a significant publication. Similarly, Portland Art Museum developed its Contemporary Northwest Art Awards. Each of these efforts demonstrated the strength and energy of the region's visual artists and local curators' newly engaged critical approaches.

The confluence of colleges and universities, commercial galleries, groups such as the Northwest Designer Craftsmen, and the attention of local curators provided a critical mass for engagement with regional concerns. The early genesis of such commitment was noted by art critic Lucy Lippard in 1976: "I conclude that there is plenty of energy, plenty of visual intelligence and plenty of up-to-date art knowledge in the Northwest. The real problem, here as in other places isolated from the art markets of the world, will be how to survive, how to maintain that energy, how to set up situations which nourish and focus it."[30]

The arc from the regional to the international and then toward a dynamic synthesis speaks of the health and growing confidence of the region's artists and institutions and a reinvestment in the importance of meaningful self-assessment. Artists have decided that the stories of the region and the people who inhabit it are valuable subjects. Personal experience of a place and its culture produces authentic meaning for people who collect and see such work. Portland-based critic Jon Raymond conveyed this newfound optimism among artists working in Portland, writing sardonically that "despite the city's considerable drawbacks as an art town (its snide, nearly subliterate critics and undereducated collector pool are two big ones), it seems like a good time to be in Portland right now. I think this is the year we're really going to see some progress in our project of building civilization on the Willamette, at long last."[31]

Raymond's qualified optimism hints at the possibility of blending cosmopolitanism, or "the international style," with a strong willingness to acknowledge the importance of particular geographies in art production. This sets in motion an intractable predicament for artists working in the region: they are virtually always relegated to the outside by the mainstream art world by definition and geography. The critic Terry Smith explored the implications of this conundrum in 1974, referencing the Australian art critic Robert Hughes:

> Their worlds are replete with tensions between two antithetical terms: a defiant urge to localism (a claim for the possibility and validity of "making good, original art right here") and a reluctant recognition that the generative innovations in art, and the criteria for standards of "quality," "originality," "interest," "forcefulness," etc. are determined externally. Far from encouraging innocent art of naïve purity, untainted by "too much history and too much thinking," provincialism, in fact, produces highly self-conscious art "obsessed with the problem of what its identity ought to be."[32]

Similarly, Patricia Failing made an intriguing observation about the appeal of the regional:

> Here an analogy with regionalist cooking makes perfect sense: why expect a visitor to choose a Seattle beefsteak instead of the more exotic filet of salmon? A happy ending to this story thus depends on whether one makes the equivalent of beefsteak or salmon in one's art, that is, whether one makes art that alludes in some way to geographical particularities or is primarily involved with national and international styles and concepts addressed by other artists outside the region.[33]

Failing's analogy speaks to the essentialist argument that identity springs "from the soil."[34] Mention of the salmon, the totem of the Northwest, evokes the special qualities that unite this disparate region. Salmon cross ecosystems and geographical barriers. The salmon's fate ties the region's inhabitants together in a multitude of ways and magnitudes, from the nearly ubiquitous grilled salmon meal to federal regulations and international treaty obligations.

The centrality of the landscape as the primary factor in regional identity cannot be understated or ignored. The quality of light, the taste and purity of the water, and the bounty of the land are felt to the core. The environment is the great equalizer. Climate affects all residents with the same conditions simultaneously—specifically, we all complain about the seemingly endless gray and drizzle. Topographical attractions like Mount Rainier are celebrated and enjoyed. Geographical hindrances—such as the distance from East Coast power centers like New York City and Washington, DC—generate another societal bond.

The reception of two recent films, Vanessa Renwick's *Mighty Tacoma* (p. 213) and Matt McCormick's *The Great Northwest* (p. 212), illuminates the allure of the region's history, mystery, and idiosyncrasies for the mainstream art world.[35] In 2012, the Centre Pompidou screened *Mighty Tacoma* and the Museum of Modern Art, New York, screened *The Great Northwest*. Both artists showcase the natural beauty of the region and the complex interactions that inhabitants experience, including residents' unresolved relationship with the past and the legacy of extractive industries. Such works allow viewers to experience a distillation of the frontier, proof of the edges of the contemporary art world.

Yet, this success does not come without limits. Patricia Failing noted that artists working in time-based media such as film and video are more easily able to capture the attention of the mainstream:

> The New York art world has a continuing appetite for exoticism that draws in a certain amount of work by "outsiders." As many contemporary theorists have recognized, however, the art of the exotic outsider is almost always equated with marginality, not with serious achievement. Regional and ethnic art can offer critics and curators a temporary escape from the real business of creating art history, but it is rarely the stuff out of which that history is actually made. Exoticism thus holds regional artists in a double bind from which only a few, many of them artists who work in new media, have managed an escape to broader recognition.[36]

After more than a century, the cycle of interest in regionalism has returned. Like Mark Tobey's white writing, with its beauty, universal symbolism, and "spiritual purity," the works of this current generation of Northwest artists offer an "unspoiled" aesthetic response to a larger audience. These artists' works are steeped in the contemporary vocabularies of film and new media but with a straight-forward approach that belies their complexity. *Mighty Tacoma* and *The Great Northwest* both offer familiar stereotypes to the broader world but dazzle in their sophisticated handling of the contemporary moment.

Other factors have influenced the reception of such work both in the Northwest and outside the region. Key regional artists have successfully infused difference and energy into the quickly evolving trends in New York. Artists, collectors, and institutions have been willing to consider works about the diversity of the region's people, stories, and geographies. And artists have had the confidence and fortified willingness to embrace the regional and tell the stories of this place (demonstrating "locavorism," in the parlance of foodies).

Although artists such as Robert Colescott (p. 74) and Roger Shimomura (p. 154) began this exploration decades ago, this kind of art has become a vital expression of the richness of the Northwest experience. Artists such as Shaun Peterson (p. 182) and Marvin Oliver (p. 170) express their cultural traditions in a vocabulary created with new media and new energy. Arnold J. Kemp (p. 155) brings voice to the African American experience and confronts racial enmity. Nancy Worden speaks directly to a feminist perspective. Keith Lewis (p. 177) preserves his experience as a gay man struggling through the darkest years of the AIDS crisis. Together, these voices represent the multifaceted totality of the Northwest.

The 10th Northwest Biennial at Tacoma Art Museum in early 2012 deliberately showcased this diversity.[37] By dissolving a singular "Northwest style" into a multitude of practices and aesthetics, regional artists have the ability to reflect the enormous diversity and spirit of the region. Only through the Biennial's sprawling range of process, conceptual foundations, and imagery could the region and its artistic identity be encapsulated accurately—at least in part. Art historian Donald B. Kuspit posited that such fragmentation is a vital part of cultural identity, particularly for areas outside New York: "Regionalism implies pluralism, cosmopolitanism represents the opposing theory of assimilation. The 'cardinal assumption' of any pluralism is 'that the persistence and solidarity of ethnic minorities is essential to democracy.' If one reads 'regional' for 'ethnic' one sees the situation: if there is to be democracy—and this is the all-American issue—there must be regional art."[38]

Given our current state of transnational global capitalism, instantaneous communications, ever-widening social networks, and the market-driven interest in contemporary art, the impulse toward regional subjects and themes seems counterintuitive. Yet, the regional offers authentic expression of shared experience. Blogger Edward Winkleman commented on the attraction of such art: "And then it hit me, that this feeling was a unique appeal of artwork that we would classify as 'regionalist,' and not just representational regionalism, but of artwork created in and reflecting the lifestyle and mind set of a subsection of the world better than any of the international, universal work out there ever could."[39]

The story of contemporary Northwest art traces the cycles of interest for and confidence in regional identity. As artists become refamiliarized and fascinated with regionalism, seeking to explore opportunities and themes, the types and forms of art change accordingly with the zeitgeist and larger sphere of contemporary art. As these works become settled in time, we come to understand how Northwest artists record a vital vision of who we are, where we live, and our experiences. Because there is not a single style, Northwest artists are able to nimbly and smartly define and celebrate the region and the people who live here.

NOTES

1. Millard B. Rogers, introduction to *Northwest Art Today* (Seattle: Century 21 Exposition Inc., 1962), 9.

2. [Dorothy Seiberling], "Mystic Painters of the Northwest," *Life,* September 28, 1953, 84–89. Some collectors and scholars believe that George Tsutakawa played a critical role in establishing a unified aesthetic and artist fraternity for this group after World War II and the return to Seattle of Japanese American artists who were interned by Executive Order 1066.

3. Ibid.; Rogers, introduction to *Northwest Art Today,* 7 ("a particular muted color sense, a strong influence of the forest and the sea, and even the Oriental flavor").

4. Serge Guilbaut, *How New York Stole the Idea of Modern Art: Abstract Expressionism, Freedom, and the Cold War,* translated by Arthur Goldhammer (Chicago: University of Chicago Press, 1983).

5. Rogers, introduction to *Northwest Art Today,* 7.

6. Peter Selz with Tom Robbins, "The Pacific Northwest Today," *Art in America* 56 (November–December 1968): 98–101.

7. Ibid., 98.

8. Ibid., 101.

9. Tom Robbins, "Plague upon the Land," *Northwest Art News and Views* 1 (January–February 1970): 14.

10. Greg Lange, "Billboard Reading 'Will the Last Person Leaving Seattle—Turn Out the Lights' Appears near Sea-Tac International Airport on April 16, 1971," Historylink.org, www.historylink.org/index.cfm ?DisplayPage=output.cfm&File_Id=1287 (accessed August 5, 2012).

11. Peter T. Nesbett and Michelle DuBois, eds. *Over the Line: The Art and Life of Jacob Lawrence,* vol. 1 (Seattle: University of Washington Press in association with the Jacob Lawrence Catalogue Raisonné Project, 2000).

12. Bill Berkson, "Seattle Site," *Art in America* 74 (July 1986): 71.

13. Bill Berkson, "Report from Seattle: In the Studios," *Art in America* 74 (September 1986): 36.

14. Ned Rifkin, *Outside New York: Seattle* (New York: The New Museum, 1983), 7.

15. Bruce Guenther, *50 Northwest Artists* (San Francisco: Chronicle Books, 1983).

16. Tina Oldknow, *Pilchuck: A Glass School* (Seattle: Pilchuck Glass School in association with the University of Washington Press, 1996).

17. Rock Hushka, "A Lifetime of Inspiration: Dale Chihuly and Tacoma," in *Dale Chihuly: A Celebration*, 11–53 (New York: Abrams, 2011).

18. Lloyd E. Herman, *Looking Forward, Glancing Back: Northwest Designer Craftsmen at 50* (Bellingham, WA: Whatcom Museum of History and Art, distributed by the University of Washington Press, 2004).

19. Ron Glowen, "From the Corner," *Artweek* 26 (December 1995): 5.

20. Patricia Failing, "Sex, Landscape, and Videotapes: The Pacific Northwest," *ArtNews* 90 (December 1991): 91.

21. Ibid.

22. Ibid., 93.

23. Ivan Doig, Rock Hushka, and Patricia McDonnell, *Building Tradition: Gifts in Honor of the Northwest Art Collection* (Tacoma: Tacoma Art Museum, 2003).

24. Elizabeth Brown and Lisa Corrin, "The Mountain Is Out," *Modern Painters* Autumn 2002, 48.

25. Ibid.

26. In addition to Dale Chihuly, the list of major Northwest artists working in traditional craft media with national and international acclaim is too large to enumerate and outside the scope of this essay.

27. Ralph Rugoff, ed., *Baja to Vancouver: The West Coast and Contemporary Art* (San Francisco: CCA Wattis Institute for Contemporary Arts, 2003).

28. Randy Gragg and Matthew Stadler, eds., *Core Sample: Portland Art Now* (Astoria, OR: Clear Cut Press, 2004).

29. Tim Yohn, Monique Shira, Anna Fahey, and Helen Curtis, eds., *LAVA 2002* (Seattle: Thread, 2002).

30. Lucy Lippard, "Northwest Passage," *Art in America* 64 (July–August 1976): 63.

31. Jon Raymond, "Schisms: Less Gloom in Doom Town," *Modern Painters*, November 2006, 93.

32. Terry Smith, "The Provincialism Problem," *Artforum* 13 (September 1974): 56.

33. Patricia Failing, "Regional Indulgences," *Reflex* 3 (May–June 1989): 7.

34. John M. Findlay, "A Fishy Proposition: Regional Identity in the Pacific Northwest," in *Many Wests: Place, Culture, and Regional Identity*, 37–70 (Lawrence,: University Press of Kansas, 1997); John M. Findlay, "Something in the Soil? Literature and Regional Identity in the 20th-Century Pacific Northwest," *Pacific Northwest Quarterly* 97 (Fall 2006): 179–89. See also V. L. O. Chittick, ed., *Northwest Harvest: A Regional Stock-Taking* (New York: Macmillan, 1948).

35. Tacoma Art Museum commissioned *Mighty Tacoma* as part of the exhibition *Mighty Tacoma: Photographic Portrait 2012* to commemorate the museum's 75th anniversary.

36. Failing, "Regional Indulgences," 7.

37. Rock Hushka and Renato Rodrigues da Silva, *The 10th Northwest Biennial* (Tacoma: Tacoma Art Museum, 2012).

38. Donald B. Kuspit, "Regionalism Reconsidered," *Art in America* 64 (July–August 1976): 67.

39. Edward Winkleman, "My Epiphany about Regionalism," www.edwardwinkleman.com (accessed May 2, 2012).

Selected Works
from the Collection

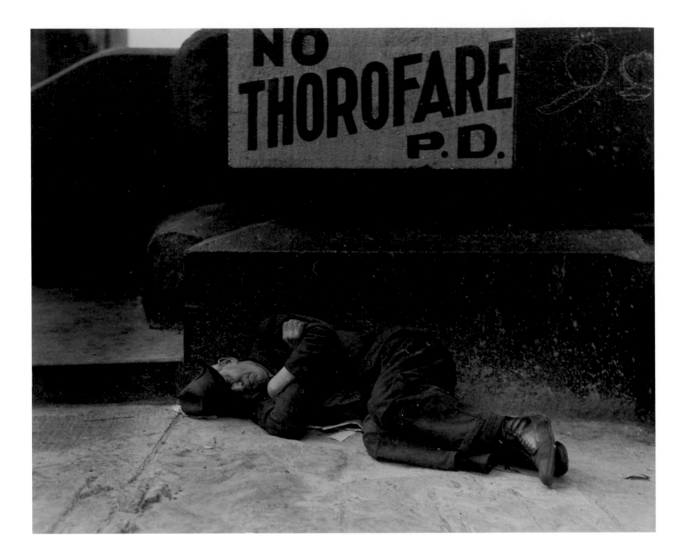

IMOGEN CUNNINGHAM
BORN PORTLAND, OREGON, 1883
DIED SAN FRANCISCO, CALIFORNIA,
1976

*Under the Queensboro
Bridge,* 1934
Gelatin silver print
5½ × 6¾ inches (14 × 17.1 cm)

Gift of the Aloha Club, 2003.1

Imogen Cunningham's early works were soft-focused compositions based on poetry and literature and influenced by Japanese aesthetics. After relocating to California, she began to concentrate on straight photography, that is, pictures that were not dependent on technical manipulation in the darkroom. A number are considered documentary, capturing social conditions and concerns of the period. In contrast to the glamour and power of the magazine photos she was shooting at the same time, this straightforward and poignant image of a homeless man encapsulates the despair and poverty that spread across the country during the 1930s' economic depression.

IMOGEN CUNNINGHAM

On Mount Rainier 8, 1915
Gelatin silver print
8½ × 6¾ inches (21.6 × 17.1 cm)

Promised gift of Shari and
John Behnke

On Mount Rainier 9, 1915
Gelatin silver print
6¾ × 8½ inches (17.1 × 21.6 cm)

Promised gift of Shari and
John Behnke

Untitled, circa 1913–15
Platinum print
9¼ × 7⅜ inches (23.5 × 18.7 cm)

Museum purchase, 2000.6

AMBROSE PATTERSON
BORN DAYLESFORD, VICTORIA,
  AUSTRALIA, 1877
DIED SEATTLE, WASHINGTON, 1966

Point Lobos, circa 1917–18
Oil on canvas
42 × 60 inches (106.7 × 152.4 cm)

Museum purchase in honor of
Wendell L. Ott, 1992.22

The evolution of Ambrose Patterson's work follows a trajectory through many of the major movements in modern art. His early images from Paris reflect his academic realist training but rapidly transition to an interest in impressionism. In his later works Patterson experimented with cubism and elements of abstraction. *Point Lobos* combines the loose, broken brushwork of impressionism with the high-toned expressive color of postimpressionism. Patterson's hybrid style in this work embodies the characteristics ascribed to the California coast—energetic, passionate, and forward thinking—that made it an increasingly popular artistic destination during this period.

AMBROSE PATTERSON

*Composition Four
    Figures,* 1931
Oil on canvas
25⅛ × 30⅛ inches (63.8 × 76.5 cm)

Gift of the Bellevue Art Museum,
1998.26.2

WAYNE ALBEE
BORN ST. PAUL, MINNESOTA, 1882
DIED SAN DIEGO, CALIFORNIA, 1937

Portrait of the Dancer
Evangeline Edwards,
circa 1922
Tinted gelatin silver print
6¼ × 4⅜ inches (15.9 × 11.1 cm)

Gift of David F. Martin and
Dominic A. Zambito, 2009.15.10

Wayne Albee was one of the Northwest's leading pictorialist photographers. An artistic movement that started in the late 19th century, pictorialism was dedicated to exploring the painterly qualities of photography. Albee exhibited his work in national and international pictorialist photography salons and won numerous awards. He was particularly known for his portraits of modern dancers, including Anna Pavlova (1881–1931), Ted Shawn (1891–1972), and Ruth St. Denis (1879–1968), all three of whom he came to know through his work at the photography studio of Ella McBride (1862–1965) and the studio's connection to the Cornish School of Allied Arts (now Cornish College of the Arts), Seattle. Evangeline Edwards (dates unknown), the subject of this photograph, had a successful career on Broadway as a dancer and actress.

ELLA MCBRIDE
BORN ALBIA, IOWA, 1862
DIED SEATTLE, WASHINGTON, 1965

Reverie, circa 1925
Silver chloride print
9½ × 7½ inches (24.1 × 19.1 cm)

Gift of Richard Anderson and
Martin-Zambito Fine Art, 2002.15.8

Ella McBride was a pictorialist photographer, manipulating her photographic negatives and using artistic compositions and soft focus to create painterly images. Portraits, still lifes, and figurative works were her primary subjects. Her studio had a close relationship with the Cornish School of Allied Arts in Seattle (now Cornish College of the Arts), where she photographed many important visiting dancers and musicians. She also created portraits of fellow artists, such as this image of Japanese sculptor and painter Ryumon Yasuda (1891–1965), who visited Seattle in the early 1920s. McBride did not begin exhibiting her photographs until later in life. Starting around 1920 she began entering work in both national and international salons, quickly building a solid reputation. She also joined and exhibited with the Seattle Camera Club in the mid- to late 1920s. McBride continued to photograph and run her studio until she retired at the age of 91.

YUKIO MORINAGA
BORN YAMAGUCHI PREFECTURE,
JAPAN, 1888
DIED TACOMA, WASHINGTON, 1968

Rainy Street, circa 1925
Gelatin silver print
13⅝ × 10 inches (34.6 × 25.4 cm)

Gift of Jacky Randall and Knut
Ringen, 2012.1.4

Yukio Morinaga was a pictorialist photographer, interested in achieving painterly effects in his photographs. By choosing to photograph in certain weather or light conditions, and becoming a master at capturing or creating subtle tonal changes in his images, he produced evocative images, both lovely and haunting. An immigrant to Seattle in 1907, he fell in love with the city and chose it as his primary subject, photographing its streets, waterfronts, and neighborhoods, as in this image near Pioneer Square.

MYRA WIGGINS
BORN SALEM, OREGON, 1869
DIED SEATTLE, WASHINGTON, 1956

Dethroned, circa 1921
Silver chloride print
8½ × 6¼ inches (21.6 × 15.9 cm)

Gift of David F. Martin and
Dominic A. Zambito, 2009.15.11

Myra Wiggins moved fluidly between painting and photography, often using the subject of a work in one medium as inspiration for another. This image is from a series of Dutch genre scenes that Wiggins created using models in period costumes and fabricated interiors. These soft-focus images are in a style known as pictorialism, a late 19th-century movement committed to exploring and promoting the artistic potential of photography. Through composition, lighting, and darkroom manipulation, pictorialists strove to demonstrate how photographs could be as creatively challenging as a painting.

Glacier Inferno,
date unknown
Gelatin silver print
9½ × 13¾ inches (24.1 × 34.9 cm)

Museum purchase with funds from
a gift of Jared FitzGerald, 2011.19.2

KYO KOIKE
BORN SHIMANE PREFECTURE,
   JAPAN, 1878
DIED SEATTLE, WASHINGTON, 1947

Between Clouds,
date unknown
Gelatin silver print
9⅞ × 7¾ inches (25.1 × 19.7 cm)

Museum purchase with funds from
a gift of Jared FitzGerald, 2011.19.1

Kyo Koike's prominence as a photographer was based on his eloquent pictorialist images of the Northwest. Among his many interests, he was a naturalist and mountaineer, and his pictures often capture the natural wonders he encountered on his hikes and expeditions as well as juxtapositions of the natural and man-made. His pictorialist images are soft-toned and moody, offering moments for deep contemplation. In some of his writings, Koike noted that his Japanese heritage influenced his compositions, leading him to prefer images that left elements to the imagination of the viewer rather than being strictly descriptive. In *Between Clouds* the viewer is enveloped by sea and sky, set adrift from the world and its concerns to meditate on the beauties of nature.

FRANK ASAKICHI KUNISHIGE

BORN AGENOSHO, YAMAGUCHI PREFECTURE, JAPAN, 1878
DIED SEATTLE, WASHINGTON, 1960

Untitled, date unknown
Gelatin silver print on Textura Tissue
8⅞ × 6 inches (22.5 × 15.2 cm)

Museum purchase with funds from a gift of Jared FitzGerald, 2011.19.3

Frank Kunishige was best known for his sensitive and evocative figurative images, though he also photographed still lifes and urban scenes. Like his pictorialist colleagues, he preferred to use gradations of shading and soft focus to create dreamy, otherworldly images. He was a master at subtly varying tonality to achieve his desired light effects. In this image, careful toning is used to model every aspect of the figure, including minor details such as the back of the woman's arm and the sole of her foot. Kunishige also developed his own photographic printing paper made from Japanese rice paper called Textura Tissue. The very thin textured paper added additional depth and surface variation to his works.

VIRNA HAFFER
BORN AURORA, ILLINOIS, 1899
DIED TACOMA, WASHINGTON, 1974

Tilley-O, circa 1928
Gelatin silver print
7⅛ inches (18.1 cm), diameter

Gift of Jacky Randall and Knut
Ringen, 2012.1.3

Virna Haffer experimented with and mastered a variety of photographic styles and techniques throughout her career, creating images that can be categorized as pictorialist, surrealist, documentary, straight, or modernist. She further manipulated her images in the darkroom by altering and combining negatives and using equipment such as her enlarger to create striking new works. *Tilley-O* was one of her earlier experiments using multiple negatives. After taking a series of photographs, Haffer selected and arranged multiple images to create this surrealist composite portrait, an image as multi-faceted as its subject the Tacoma arts patron and enthusiast, Erna Tilley (1887–1982).

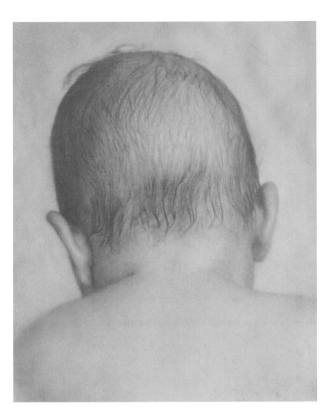

VIRNA HAFFER

Rattlesnake Grass,
  circa 1960–69
Photogram
13¾ × 10¼ inches (34.9 × 26 cm)

Gift of John Butler, 2007.46.1

His First Growth, 1923
Gelatin silver print
9⅜ × 7⅜ inches (23.8 × 18.7 cm)

Gift of Jacky Randall and Knut
Ringen, 2012.1.2

FAY CHONG

BORN CANTON, CHINA, 1912
DIED SEATTLE, WASHINGTON, 1973

South End Storage,
circa 1942

Watercolor and Chinese ink on
rice paper
12⅝ × 18¾ inches (32.1 × 47.6 cm)

Gift of Safeco Insurance, a member of the Liberty Mutual Group,
and Washington Art Consortium,
2010.6.30

Fay Chong's works blend influences from his native China and his studies in the United
States. Though he immigrated to Seattle as a child, he returned to China several times as
an adult to study calligraphy and ink painting. During the 1930s and early 1940s, when
South End Storage was created, he was employed by the Works Progress Administration's
Federal Art Project to create prints and paintings of everyday life in Seattle and the sur-
rounding area. This work is characteristic, combining thin, clear washes of watercolor and
fluid, expressive ink lines.

KENJIRO NOMURA

BORN GIFU, GIFU PREFECTURE,
   JAPAN, 1896
DIED SEATTLE, WASHINGTON, 1956

Puget Sound, circa 1933
Oil on canvas
20½ × 24½ inches (52.1 × 62.2 cm)

Gift of Mr. and Mrs. Cyril A. Spinola,
1992.8

Kenjiro Nomura painted representational images but used modernist ideas about composition, spatial construction, and form to structure his works. His palette is generally rather muted and earth-toned, capturing the watery skies, lush plant life, and often muddy environs of the Northwest. Nomura focused particularly on Seattle's neighborhoods and the rural landscape just outside the city. A number of the farms he painted were owned by fellow Japanese immigrants. *Puget Sound* captures a view in the hilly Seattle neighborhood now known as the International District, an area that Nomura painted frequently.

MARGARET CAMFFERMAN
BORN ROCHESTER, MINNESOTA, 1881
DIED EVERETT, WASHINGTON, 1964

Untitled, 1935
Oil on artist's board
25⅛ × 29½ inches (63.8 × 74.9 cm)

Gift of Maureen Duryee, 2009.9.5

Margaret Camfferman began experimenting with modernist ideas long before many of her Northwest artist contemporaries. She embraced the move away from realistic painting to artworks that manipulated space, color, technique, and subject to convey a variety of meanings. She was particularly influenced by the work of postimpressionist artists, including Paul Cézanne (1839–1906), and cubists such as her instructor André Lhote (1885–1962). In this colorful landscape, the shadows and shapes of the mountains in the background have become stylized geometric blocks of color and the rows of crops a carefully arranged pattern of greens.

PETER CAMFFERMAN
BORN THE HAGUE, NETHERLANDS, 1890
DIED LANGLEY, WASHINGTON, 1957

Untitled, circa 1930s
Oil on artist's board
26 × 30¼ inches (66 × 76.8 cm)

Gift of Maureen Duryee, 2009.9.2

Peter Camfferman was an early modernist artist in the Northwest, avant-garde even among other forward-looking painters, such as his colleagues in the progressive Group of Twelve, a loose association of Seattle artists interested in modern art. The flattened picture plane, loose brushwork, and abbreviated detail in this painting are all modernist strategies designed to focus the viewer on more than just the picture's subject. A student of the synchromist painter Stanton MacDonald-Wright (1890–1973), Camfferman absorbed MacDonald-Wright's interest in the emotional power of color. He often used color expressively to suggest a particular mood or feeling evoked by his subject.

WILLIAM GIVLER
BORN OMAHA, NEBRASKA, 1908
DIED PORTLAND, OREGON, 2000

Window Washers, 1935
Oil on canvas
27 × 37 inches (68.6 × 94 cm)

Gift of Safeco Insurance, a member of the Liberty Mutual Group, and Washington Art Consortium to Whatcom Museum and Tacoma Art Museum, 2010.6.42

William Givler's paintings combine the Northwest's muted palette and occasional flashes of bright color with loose, expressive brushwork. In his later career he focused almost exclusively on landscapes, often favoring images set along the Oregon coast. However, in his earlier works he painted a variety of subjects, most often scenes from the daily lives of everyday people, a theme picked up by many modernist artists in the early 20th century. In *Window Washers* he focuses on laborers at work, capturing the dynamic energy of their movements through curving lines and gestures.

PEGGY STRONG
BORN ABERDEEN, WASHINGTON, 1912
DIED SAN FRANCISCO, CALIFORNIA, 1956

Young Man with Trowel,
circa 1939
Oil on canvas
36¼ × 29¼ inches (92.1 × 74.3 cm)

Gift of Catharine Strong Sammons, 2001.1

Though Washington painter Peggy Strong most often focused on representational images of daily life, she also painted abstractly and was known for both easel paintings and murals. *Young Man with Trowel* blends elements of realism with abstraction, a common combination in the art of this period. The sitter's facial features and clothes are carefully rendered but the bench on which he is perched seems too shallow for sitting and the background is pure expressionist painting.

Rodeo, 1945–46
Color silkscreen
12 1/16 × 14 inches
(30.6 × 35.6 cm)

Gift of the artist and Martin-
Zambito Fine Art, 1993.6.1

**YVONNE TWINING
HUMBER**
BORN NEW YORK, NEW YORK, 1907
DIED REDMOND, WASHINGTON, 2004

Carnival, 1946
Color silkscreen
11 1/2 × 13 7/8 inches (29.2 × 35.2 cm)

Gift of David F. Martin, Dominic
Zambito, and the artist, 1999.11.1

Yvonne Twining Humber was one of the first hard-edged realist painters in the Northwest. A transplant from the East Coast, she made her reputation working for the Federal Art Project (FAP) in Boston in the 1930s. The FAP encouraged artists to focus on American Scene painting, images from everyday life, both rural and urban. Humber continued to capture those kinds of scenes when she moved to the Northwest. Her images are characterized by lively color, expressive line, and a keen eye for significant detail. Works like *Carnival* and *Rodeo* reveal her particular flair for capturing the sights and sounds of public gatherings.

JULIUS TWOHY

TRIBAL AFFILIATION: UTE
BORN WHITE ROCKS, UTE RESERVA-
TION, UTAH, 1902
DIED 1986, LOCATION UNKNOWN

New Vision, 1933
Charcoal on paper
23½ × 17½ inches (59.7 × 44.5 cm)

Museum purchase, 2009.16

Like many of his contemporaries, Julius Twohy painted a number of American Scene images, that is, images of American daily life. These images are representational but contain modernist elements such as expressive color, reduced detail, and compressed space. He also created compositions such as *New Vision* that were primarily symbolic rather than realistic. In many works Twohy used Native American symbols and other graphic elements to create dramatic, stylized designs. The swastika at the bottom center of this image was used by Native Americans to suggest natural cycles, such as the movements of the sun and moon, and the circle of life.

THOMAS HANDFORTH
BORN TACOMA, WASHINGTON, 1897
DIED PASADENA, CALIFORNIA, 1948

Self Portrait, 1947
Graphite on paper
17⅞ × 15 inches (45.4 × 38.1 cm),
sheet

Gift of Mrs. Brian Shera and
Edward C. and Tim Shera, sons,
1987.1.1

Thomas Handforth was an extremely prolific artist, and large groups of his work can be found in museum and library collections throughout the Northwest as well as in numerous private collections. He worked primarily as an illustrator in a lively linear style, but in portraits and some of his prints he used detail and shading to create subtly evocative images. The way in which he chose to crop this self-portrait to create a disembodied head and his direct, rather challenging gaze give this picture a unique, slightly surreal edge.

DOROTHY DOLPH JENSEN
BORN FOREST GROVE, OREGON, 1895
DIED SEATTLE, WASHINGTON, 1977

Through Two Mirrors,
circa 1930
Oil on canvas board
22½ × 18¼ inches (57.2 × 46.4 cm)

Gift of Anita Carmin and
Lloyd Carmin, 2010.15.2

Dorothy Dolph Jensen's paintings blend expressive color with loose yet descriptive brush-work. Her compositions are carefully structured and dynamic even when the subject is static. She was particularly adept at the modernist art of modeling forms with subtle varia-tions and juxtapositions of color rather than using line. In this self-portrait, *Through Two Mirrors,* she proudly depicts herself as a working artist posed in her painting smock, brush in hand and surrounded by other examples of her work. The painting also subtly acknowl-edges through its title that this is how she wanted to be perceived by others: by using two mirrors she was able to paint herself as others saw her rather than the reversed image she would have of herself in a single mirror.

WALTER ISAACS
BORN GILLESPIE, ILLINOIS, 1886
DIED SEATTLE, WASHINGTON, 1964

Untitled, circa 1940s
Oil and graphite on paper
15 × 19⅜ inches (38.1 × 49.2 cm)

Gift of Paul I. Gingrich Jr. in
memory of Pernilla K. Johnson,
2000.38

Walter Isaacs was a member of the Group of Twelve, a loose association of Seattle artists in the 1910s and 1920s interested in modern art. His focus differed from his better-known and more mystical contemporaries of the Northwest school, who were more interested in regional environmental influences. Isaacs was a devotee of modernist painting, influenced particularly by his studies in Paris. In this untitled interior, Isaacs stretches the cubist sense of space. Figure and objects float on an unspecified flat ground. The use of gentle pastel colors creates a tension with the very rough handling of shape, tone, and line.

WALTER ISAACS

Horses in Paddock, 1945
Oil on board
27⅝ × 31⅝ inches (70.2 × 80.3 cm)

Gift of Safeco Insurance, a member of the Liberty Mutual Group, and Washington Art Consortium, 2010.6.52

Z. VANESSA HELDER
BORN LYNDEN, WASHINGTON, 1904
DIED LOS ANGELES, CALIFORNIA,
1968

Water Tower, 1939
Watercolor on paper
17½ × 22 inches (44.5 × 55.9 cm)

Gift of the Aloha Club in honor of
Tacoma Art Museum's 75th Anniversary, 2011.1.1

Zama Vanessa Helder's work is often identified with a style known as precisionism for the sharp, linear edges used to define objects. Precisionist images celebrate America's then-fledgling industrial and urban age and the crisp geometry of its factories, skyscrapers, bridges, and other architectural wonders. Helder took this style to new heights by working in watercolor, creating works that radiate clear color and showing a rare talent for tightly controlling a medium known for its fluidity and soft, blurry lines. This image was painted in eastern Washington while she was teaching at the Federal Art Project's Spokane Art Center.

CARL HALL
BORN WASHINGTON, DC, 1921
DIED SALEM, OREGON, 1996

*Thunderbird Wings
(Alert Bay Cormorant),*
1975
Gouache and tissue paper on
illustration board
35½ × 54½ inches (90.2 × 138.4 cm)

Gift of the Carl Hall Family through
Bill Rhoades, 2012.3

Carl Hall was a prolific painter whose primary subject was the Oregon landscape, particularly the Willamette Valley and the Pacific coast. Based on his travels, he also painted locations throughout the Northwest and Alaska, including this image from British Columbia. His works often have a surrealist edge, as he combines crisp line and detail with unusual viewpoints, illusionistic surface texture, and unexpected juxtapositions. In this work, Hall added tissue paper to the surface and then painted over it with watercolor and gouache to heighten the atmospheric effects and add an element of abstraction.

MARGARET DE PATTA
BORN TACOMA, WASHINGTON, 1903
DIED OAKLAND, CALIFORNIA, 1964

Untitled, circa 1955–60
Sterling silver, rock, and pearl
3¼ × ¹⁄₁₆ × ³⁄₁₆ inches
(8.3 × 0.2 cm × 0.5 cm)

Gift of Ramona Solberg and Betty
Swift, 2001.9

Margaret De Patta was the first West Coast jeweler to work with modernist design ideas, notably simple, often architecturally based forms, and clean lines. She was particularly influenced by the utilitarian and industrially inflected principles of the constructivists and Bauhaus design. She created crisp, stylish jewelry designed to shift and change with its wearer's movements. She also worked with nontraditional gemstones and unique cuts. This simple, elegant pin celebrates the beauty of everyday stones and the subtle, structural importance of silver.

RUTH PENINGTON
BORN COLORADO SPRINGS,
COLORADO, 1905
DIED SEATTLE, WASHINGTON, 1998

Untitled, 1971
Silver and ermine tails
9½ × 10 × 3⁄16 inches
(24.1 × 25.4 × 0.5 cm)

Gift of Anne Gould Hauberg,
1999.16

As one of the early leaders of the studio art jewelry movement in the Northwest, Ruth Penington is remembered for her rigorous command of traditional techniques and her emphasis on vibrant design. She often combined precious materials with nonprecious objects such as beach pebbles and wire or, as in this necklace, with substances that offered a striking textural contrast to the silver framework of her necklaces, rings, and bracelets. One of the hallmarks of her jewelry is sleek and elegant design based on modernist, geometric forms.

JAMES CASTLE
BORN GARDEN VALLEY, IDAHO, 1899
DIED BOISE, IDAHO, 1977

Untitled, date unknown
Soot on paper
9¾ × 9¾ inches (24.8 × 24.8 cm),
sheet

Gift of Constance Speth, 2004.25.5

Folk artist James Castle drew inspiration for his works from his day-to-day environment as well as from magazines, catalogues, advertisements, and newspapers. His compositions often incorporate fragments of the logos, designs, and other motifs printed on the found papers he used. Though Castle worked with a sharpened stick and soot as his primary materials, his drawings often exhibit clear detail and subtle shading. Others are more naïve and simplistic. Castle was self-taught, learning perspective, shading, and other techniques through observation and copying of other artworks. In this composition he repeats the same image but treats it as if it were a puzzle piece, reorienting and reinserting it into his hexagonal design.

MAUDE KERNS
BORN PORTLAND, OREGON, 1876
DIED EUGENE, OREGON, 1965

Yang and Yin, 1943
Oil on canvas
24½ × 21¾ inches (62.2 × 55.2 cm)

Gift of Leslie Brockelbank through
Bill Rhoades, 2007.51

The geometric shapes in this painting are part of the vocabulary for a particular form of abstraction called non-objective art. The style originated with the artist Vassily Kandinsky (1866–1944), who believed abstractions should make no reference to the physical world but should instead express spiritual concepts. Maude Kerns was one of the few Northwest artists who practiced non-objective painting. Through her ties to New York's Museum of Non-Objective Painting (now the Solomon R. Guggenheim Museum) and her decades as a teacher at the University of Oregon, she helped bring avant-garde artistic ideas to generations of Northwest art students and the art-loving public.

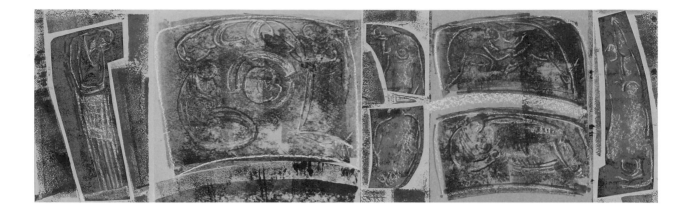

GUY ANDERSON

BORN EDMONDS, WASHINGTON,
1906
DIED LA CONNER, WASHINGTON,
1998

*Cultural Fragments:
Han · Haida · Greek,*
1962

Acrylic paint, chalk, and glue
on paper
15³⁄₁₆ × 40¼ inches
(38.6 × 102.2 cm)

Gift of William S. and Janice Street,
1997.24.4

This work is a study for the large mural, *Cultural Fragments,* by Guy Anderson currently housed in McCaw Hall, home of the Seattle Opera, as part of the City of Seattle Portable Works Collection. The study incorporates design motifs from three of the world's great cultures: Asia, represented by the Han dynasty in China (206 BC–AD 220); the Haida, Native people from the Northwest coast, representing the peoples of the First Nations; and ancient Greece, the cornerstone of Western civilization. Anderson often used symbols in his work to weave social, moral, and philosophical messages into his compositions. Here, his work addresses the universal human connections underlying diverse cultures.

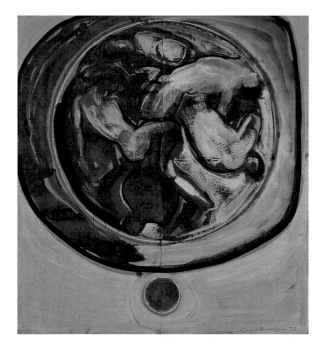

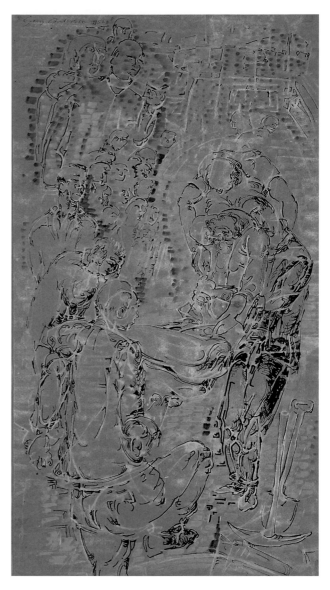

GUY ANDERSON

Circle of Life, 1972
Oil on paper
87½ × 80 inches (222.3 × 203.2 cm)

Gift of the Aloha Club, 1974.3

Deposition of a Miner, 1952
Watercolor, ink, and chalk on paper
23¾ × 13 inches (60.3 × 33 cm)

Gift of Mr. and Mrs. L. T. Murray, Sr., 1967.1

KENNETH CALLAHAN
BORN SPOKANE, WASHINGTON, 1905
DIED SEATTLE, WASHINGTON, 1986

Cascades, late 1930s
Gouache on paper
21 × 31⅜ inches (53.3 × 79.7 cm)

Gift of the Aloha Club, 1971.10

Kenneth Callahan's paintings are imbued with the expressive energy exemplified by *Cascades*. With vigorous, broad brushwork and clever manipulation of object scale and exaggerated perspective, he shows us a scene in the Cascade Mountains that captures the sheer power of the landscape. In his earliest paintings, Callahan recorded the scenes he knew best: of loggers and laborers and the Northwest landscape in a rough-hewn figurative style. His later works became more abstract and metaphysical in nature, designed to inspire contemplation in the viewer.

KENNETH CALLAHAN

*Preliminary Study for
  UN Security Council
  Competition,* 1959–60
Tempera on board
28¾ × 70 inches (73 × 177.8 cm)

Gift of the Bellevue Art Museum,
1998.26.15

MORRIS GRAVES
BORN FOX VALLEY, OREGON, 1910
DIED LOLETA, CALIFORNIA, 2001

Chalice Holding the
Stimson Mill, 1936
Oil on canvas
67 × 39½ inches (170.2 × 100.3 cm)

Gift of Robert Ohashi, Ross Ohashi,
and Arnold Ohashi, 2007.14

In the 1930s Morris Graves's paintings reflected his concerns about the state of the rapidly changing world. In this canvas he depicted the Stimson Mill (then located just outside of Ballard in Seattle) isolated in the cup of a chalice. Graves adapted surrealist symbolism to make a powerful commentary on the negative impact of the rapid economic and political changes in Seattle. He emphasized his point by contrasting the gritty factory to the purity of fallow fields. Graves was one of several Northwest artists to experiment with surrealism, including Malcolm Roberts (1913–1990) and Louis Bunce (1907–1983).

MORRIS GRAVES

Autumn Still Life, 1952
Oil on canvas
31½ × 48½ inches (80 × 123.2 cm)

Gift of Marianne Johnson in honor
of Morris Graves, 2006.35

MARK TOBEY
BORN CENTERVILLE, WISCONSIN, 1890
DIED BASEL, SWITZERLAND, 1976

Point of Intersection,
1949
Tempera on panel
11¼ × 14 inches (28.6 × 35.6 cm)

Gift of Mr. and Mrs. Hollis Day, 1978.5

Mark Tobey's artistic interests were spiritual as well as formal. Inspired by the Bahá'í faith and Zen Buddhism, he created a unique visual vocabulary for expressing his conceptual framework. From his travels in Asia and the Middle East, Tobey became fascinated with calligraphy and Arabic script and created a style of painting he called "white writing." These paintings, which include elements from the real world, are densely packed compositions in which details, rendered in white, swirl in and through ambiguous spaces. *Point of Intersection* contains layers of landscape, figures, and fragments of buildings interwoven with a network of lines and marks.

MARK TOBEY

Northwest Fantasy, 1953
Tempera on canvas
43 × 48½ inches (109.2 × 123.2 cm)

Promised gift of Anne Gould Hauberg

PAUL HORIUCHI
BORN OISHI, YAMANASHI PREFEC-
TURE, JAPAN, 1906
DIED SEATTLE, WASHINGTON, 1999

Weathered, 1956
Collage on board
28⅛ × 34¼ inches (71.4 × 87 cm)

Gift of Paul and Bernadette
Horiuchi, 1988.1.1

Starting in the 1950s, Paul Horiuchi immersed himself in experimentation with the medium of collage, elevating it to a level beyond the purely decorative and exploring its relationship to both traditional Japanese sources and contemporary American principles of abstraction. In *Weathered*, his first collage, Horiuchi was responding to a weathered billboard in Seattle's International District, attracted by the patterns created by the peeling layers of old newspapers. He purposely rearranged the text so that the viewer is not distracted by the content but rather focuses on the colors, textures, and shapes.

PAUL HORIUCHI

Persuasiveness of
*   Antiquity,* 1966
Collage, sumi ink, paper, paint with
iridescent surface application on
six-panel screen
59½ × 128¾ inches (151.1 × 327 cm)

Promised gift of Richard Mull
and Gina Knox in honor of
Bernadette Horiuchi

LOUIS BUNCE
BORN LANDER, WYOMING, 1907
DIED PORTLAND, OREGON, 1983

Big Green, 1960
Oil on mattress ticking
71⅜ × 66 inches (181.9 × 167.6 cm)

Gift of Michele Russo, 1995.3

As an artist, Louis Bunce was a chameleon, always open to new styles and techniques. Over the course of his career, he created a prolific and varied body of work, constantly experimenting with new ideas. Like that of many artists active during the mid-20th century, Bunce's work evolved gradually from representational imagery to abstraction. When *Big Green* was created, he was deeply involved with exploring the expressive qualities of paint, color, and gesture.

LOUIS BUNCE

Pages, 1965
Oil on canvas
36 × 48 inches (91.4 × 121.9 cm)

Gift of Safeco Insurance, a member of the Liberty Mutual Group, and Washington Art Consortium, 2010.6.17

Untitled, 1969
Colored pencil on paper
5⁷⁄₁₆ × 5¾ inches (13.8 × 14.6 cm)

Gift of Robert and Shaké Sarkis, 2010.19.3

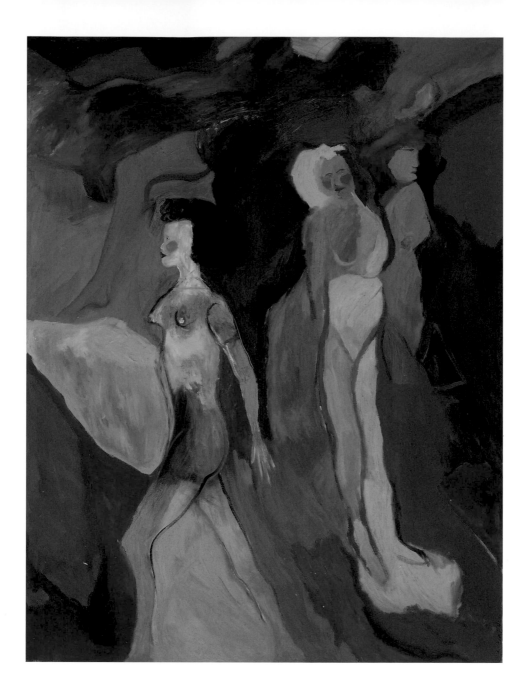

ROBERT COLESCOTT
BORN OAKLAND, CALIFORNIA, 1925
DIED TUCSON, ARIZONA, 2009

The Virgin Queen,
circa 1967
Oil on canvas
76 × 57⅝ inches (193 × 146.4 cm)

Gift of Helen Ivey, 1997.4

In 1964 Robert Colescott was awarded a teaching residency in Cairo. He became fascinated by the way symbols and iconic figures were used to convey narratives in ancient Egyptian art and created a series of works, including *The Virgin Queen,* drawing on this Egyptian vocabulary. In this work he poses his figures in the stiffly formal attitudes common to Egyptian tomb art. Though some figures are almost continuous with the colorful abstract background, his central figure, painted a distinctive white, strides purposefully toward another destiny.

BARBARA EARL THOMAS
BORN SEATTLE, WASHINGTON, 1948

The Storm Watch, 1988
Egg tempera on paper
21¾ × 29⅞ inches (55.2 × 75.9 cm)

Gift of Carol I. Bennett, 2004.34.1

In her work, Barbara Earl Thomas combines the precise, controlled medium of egg tempera with tumultuous emotional content. After Thomas's parents drowned in a fishing accident in 1988, she wrote, "It was clear that everything from then on would be defined in my life by whether it happened before or after this moment." Thomas began working on *The Storm Watch* before her parents died but finished it in the months afterward. She transformed the painting into an emotionally charged statement about security, kindness, and comfort: that within the destruction of a storm, people hold onto each other and provide unconditional support.

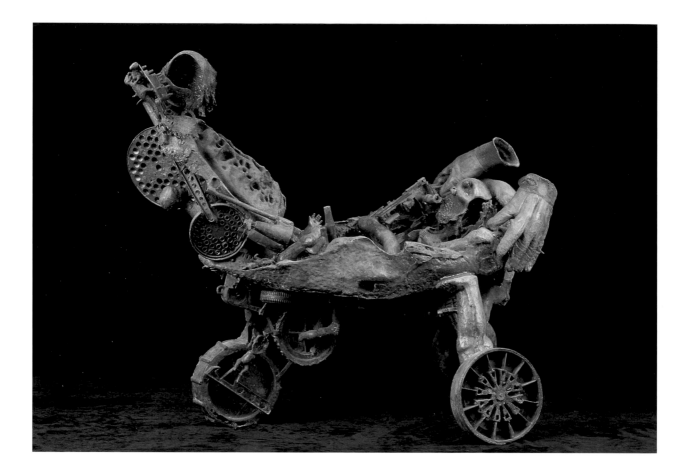

JAMES FITZGERALD
BORN SEATTLE, WASHINGTON, 1910
DIED SEATTLE, WASHINGTON, 1973

The Buggy, 1968
Bronze
31 × 27 × 38 inches
(78.7 × 68.6 × 96.5 cm)

Museum purchase, 1999.9

James FitzGerald is best remembered for his aggressive aesthetic that reflected the social turbulence of the 1960s. His works often contain a visual cacophony of symbols, forms, and rough-hewn surfaces. *The Buggy* is composed of a multitude of cast doll arms and legs that hold together a wheelbarrow-like structure made of toy ships and fighter planes as well as other machine parts. FitzGerald mounted a toy machine gun at the center of the sculpture, leaving no ambiguity that this is a war machine held together by the limbs of soldiers and civilians killed during action. FitzGerald's aggressive aesthetic and pointed symbolism speak directly to the artist's deep and lifelong antiwar sentiments.

JAMES FITZGERALD

Untitled, 1940
Oil on linen
9¾ × 12¼ inches (24.8 × 31.1 cm)

Gift of Jared and Jennifer
FitzGerald, 2004.20.2

Yankee Yente's Pony Pelt, 1967
Ceramic, pony fur, sheep fleece, and gilding
15½ × 15 × 10 inches
(39.4 × 38.1 × 25.4 cm)

Gift of Anne Gerber, 2005.6

Sprout Reed Pot, 1957
Glazed ceramic
21¾ × 3¾ × 2½ inches
(55.2 × 9.5 × 6.4 cm)

Gift of Safeco Insurance, a member of the Liberty Mutual Group, and Washington Art Consortium, 2010.6.58

HOWARD KOTTLER
BORN CLEVELAND, OHIO, 1930
DIED SEATTLE, WASHINGTON, 1989

Devil Walk, 1987
Ceramic, paint, and steel
Dimensions variable

Gift of the Howard Kottler Testamentary Trust, 1998.56 A-J

Howard Kottler was a pivotal figure in 20th-century American ceramics. An innovator, he helped change the view of ceramics from a strictly utilitarian medium to a challenging and expressive artistic form. Kottler's works from the 1950s and early 1960s reflect the predominant art world interest in abstract expressionism. In the mid-1960s he became interested in the funk art movement, appropriating images from popular culture to convey his political, social, and personal messages. Based on these works, Kottler developed a reputation for using coded images, wordplay, and biting humor—a trademark he continued to use when he began creating mixed-media sculptural ceramics and, later, slip-cast assemblages. In these later series, Kottler often incorporated surrealist elements with a nod toward conceptual art, such as the subtle and fragmented self-portrait in a cubist mode in *Devil Walk*.

alternate view

RUDY AUTIO
BORN BUTTE, MONTANA, 1926
DIED MISSOULA, MONTANA, 2007

Untitled, 1961
Ceramic and glazes
19 × 11¼ × 8½ inches (48.3 × 28.6 ×
21.6 cm)

Gift of Gene and Liz Brandzel,
1998.36

In the Northwest in the 1950s, artists began exploring the use of traditional craft media—glass, fiber, clay—to create artworks rather than solely utilitarian objects. Rudy Autio was one of the pioneers who investigated the expressive possibilities of ceramics and helped spark what is called the clay revolution. Autio's earliest vessels are traditional functional forms, but during the 1950s he began moving toward a more expressionist mode, leaving tool marks, fingerprints, gouges, cracks, and other irregularities on the surfaces of his works. He also began distorting the vessel walls and gesturally applying glazes and colors. His later works are fully sculptural, often figures molded around a central vessel shape. This work is fully expressionist in both shape and surface treatment.

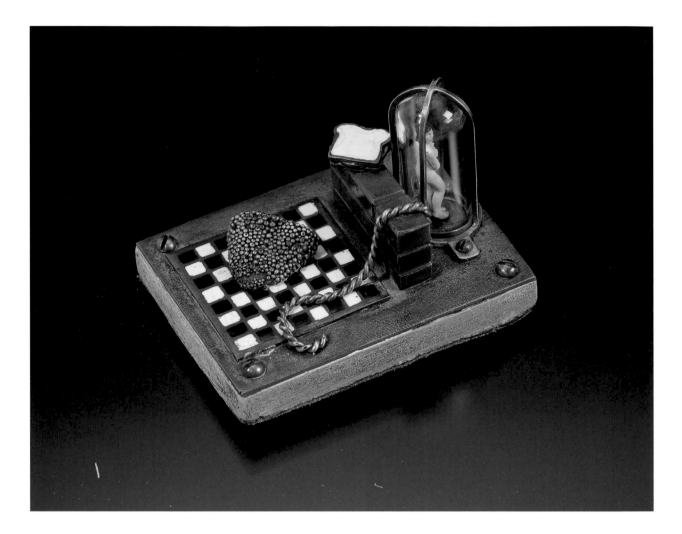

KEN CORY
BORN KIRKLAND, WASHINGTON, 1943
DIED ELLENSBURG, WASHINGTON, 1994

Monument to Katie Moon, 1971
Lead, copper, brass, silver, enamel, glass, and plastic
1⁷⁄₁₆ × 2¼ × 1¹¹⁄₁₆ inches (3.7 × 5.7 × 4.3 cm)

Gift of the Estate of Ken Cory, 1998.29.36

Ken Cory was a prominent figure in the Northwest studio art jewelry movement, creating works with a strong pop sensibility and wry sense of humor, often incorporating found objects. During the 1970s he formed an artistic collaboration called the Pencil Brothers with artist Leslie LePere (born 1946). Cory went on to produce an extensive solo body of work with influences as wide ranging as abstract expressionist assemblage, Native American symbolism, and early modernist jewelry filtered through bawdy humor, pop culture, and wordplay to create a unique and innovative personal style. Tacoma Art Museum is home to a retrospective collection of 44 of Cory's works, gift of his estate in 1998. *Monument to Katie Moon* is an homage to Kenneth Patchen's *Journal of Albion Moonlight,* a cult literary classic that explores the American psyche of the 1940s. Cory read the book as a student and was influenced by this work and others in the genre. The trapped woman and chessboard may refer to the sense of personal entrapment and political machinations that Patchen explored in his prose.

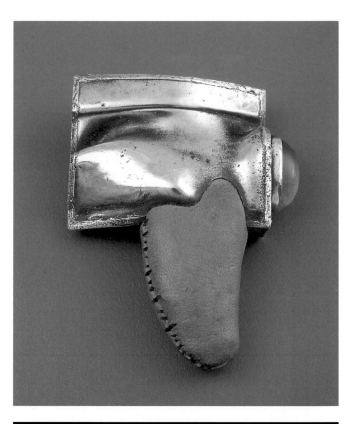

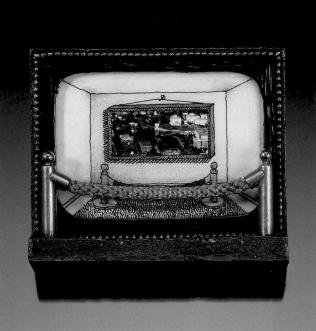

KEN CORY

Tongue, 1967
Silver, amber, and leather
2 × 1⁹⁄₁₆ × ½ inches (5.1 × 4 × 1.3 cm)

Gift of the Estate of Ken Cory,
1998.29.4

PENCIL BROTHERS

Homage to Bob Helm,
1969
Copper, brass, silver, wood, silk,
Plexiglas, and pen-and-ink drawing
on paper
1¾ × 2 × ½ inches (4.4 × 5.1 ×
1.3 cm)

Gift of Leslie LePere, 1997.26.1

WILLIAM IVEY
BORN SEATTLE, WASHINGTON, 1919
DIED SEATTLE, WASHINGTON, 1992

Blues and Whites, 1976
Oil on canvas
61 × 61 inches (154.9 × 154.9 cm)

Gift of the Aloha Club, 1977.2

William Ivey was an abstract expressionist painter who developed a highly personal style grounded in the works of his professors, Clyfford Still (1904–1980), Mark Rothko (1903–1970), and Ad Reinhardt (1913–1967) at the California School of Fine Arts (now the San Francisco Art Institute). Ivey spent most of his life in Seattle and created works inspired by observation of the real world. However, his intense immersion in the painting process transformed the original subject matter into lush abstractions that emphasize dark and light, color, and the picture plane. In Ivey's paintings, shapes seem subordinate to color in the development of spaces, and delicate neutral grays set off glowing patches of bright hues.

WILLIAM IVEY

Untitled, 1976
Oil on canvas
89¾ × 115 inches (228 × 292.1 cm)

Gift of Safeco Insurance, a member of the Liberty Mutual Group, and Washington Art Consortium, to Western Washington University and Tacoma Art Museum, 2010.6.53

JOHN FRANKLIN KOENIG
BORN SEATTLE, WASHINGTON, 1924
DIED SEATTLE, WASHINGTON, 2008

Muro-Mae, 1984
Oil on canvas
48¼ × 32¼ inches (122.6 × 81.9 cm)

Gift of Jim and Wendy Griffin,
2003.40

John Franklin Koenig was a prolific and multifaceted artist. His primary media were painting and collage, though he also worked with ceramics, glass, and photography. As a child he was fascinated with the collections at the Seattle Asian Art Museum and as an adult he made numerous trips to Japan, absorbing the culture and aesthetics and reflecting them back in his work. As an expatriate artist and gallery owner living in Paris during the 1950s to 1980s, he also was influenced by European modernist painting, attracted first to collage then to abstract painting. *Muro-Mae* is characteristic of his paintings, which combine lush, loosely brushed surfaces with collage elements and enigmatic symbols to create moody, muted images whose meanings hover just out of reach.

MARGARET TOMKINS
BORN LOS ANGELES, CALIFORNIA,
1916
DIED SEDONA, ARIZONA, 2002

Genesis, 1956
Tempera on masonite
55½ × 49 inches (141 × 124.5 cm)

Gift of Jared and Jennifer
FitzGerald, 2004.20.21

Throughout her career painter Margaret Tomkins was interested in layering and patterns, whether created by organic forms as in her earliest works or by the abstract shapes she worked with from the 1950s on. Transformation and metamorphosis also were common themes, with forms shape-shifting across her canvases, twisting and intertwining with or obscuring each other. Tomkins primarily used a limited palette of grays, whites, and earth tones, with occasional flashes of red, blue, and yellow. She developed an intricate symbolic language to express social and environmental concerns or reflect on personal experiences. *Genesis* is a complex interweaving of shapes that are both abstract and suggestive of figures and landscapes, capturing the drama of form emerging from elemental energy at a moment of creation.

GLEN ALPS

BORN LOVELAND, COLORADO, 1914
DIED SEATTLE, WASHINGTON, 1996

Collagraph #21,
date unknown
Collagraph
20¼ × 26 inches (51.4 × 66 cm)

Gift of the Estate of Glen Alps,
1999.14.3

Glen Alps was an innovative and experimental printmaker who throughout his career explored a variety of printmaking processes beyond the traditional, pushing and redefining the field. He is best known for developing a collage printmaking technique he labeled the collagraph. Objects are collaged onto a plate or other support and the resulting textured surface is then inked and printed. Though elements of collage were used in printmaking prior to Alps, he is most often misidentified as the inventor of the collagraph technique, as he extensively studied and formalized the process and was its foremost practitioner. In the 1970s he also experimented with burnt lacquer prints, a technique in which automotive lacquer was poured onto masonite and then burned away to create a design. While artist in residence at Pilchuck Glass School in 1988, he was introduced to vitreography, or glass-plate printing.

GLEN ALPS

Deer, 1945
Serigraph
8⅛ × 10½ inches (20.6 × 26.7 cm)

Gift of the Estate of Glen Alps,
1999.14.12

MANUEL IZQUIERDO
BORN MADRID, SPAIN, 1925
DIED PORTLAND, OREGON, 2009

Iberian Venus, 1983
Bronze
24⅝ × 11 × 7 inches (62.5 × 27.9 × 17.8 cm)

Gift of Sally Haley and Michele Russo, 1998.20

In his sculptural work, Manuel Izquierdo explored the use of pure geometry, the physical properties and potentials of various metals, and the balancing of weights and shapes. Though abstracted, a number of his works, like *Iberian Venus,* also reference figures in both title and substance. These simplified shapes are reminiscent of the earliest known sculptures that evoke and celebrate elemental human forms and energies. This work also references the cubist figural sculptures of Izquierdo's compatriot, the well-known Spanish artist, Pablo Picasso (1881–1973).

GEORGE TSUTAKAWA
BORN SEATTLE, WASHINGTON, 1910
DIED SEATTLE, WASHINGTON, 1997

Chimera, 1988
Bronze
18¼ × 24⅝ × 4⅛ inches
(46.4 × 62.5 × 10.5 cm)

Gift of the Aloha Club, 1989.3

George Tsutakawa's works blend Eastern and Western cultural influences in both design and subject, though he hoped to ultimately transcend specific cultural references. Both organic and abstract, his works suggest living forms. With *Chimera,* as in many of his smaller sculptures, the composition centers around an open space and evokes both figurative and totemic shapes. The word *chimera* refers to an imaginary monster or an illusion of the mind, an idea captured in the sculpture's shifting appearance.

JOSEPH GOLDBERG
BORN SEATTLE, WASHINGTON, 1947

Cobalt Violet Dark,
circa 1970
Oil and encaustic on linen
on plywood
22 × 27 inches (55.9 × 68.6 cm)

Gift of the Bellevue Art Museum,
1998.26.26

After completing his studies at the University of Washington, Joseph Goldberg embraced a reductive painting style, rejecting heavily textured, visceral gestures. He was one of the first Northwest artists to embrace this aesthetic. Because of his interest in natural forms and his tendency to paint objects suspended in an ethereal, endless ground, Goldberg is often considered an heir to the iconic Northwest painters Mark Tobey (1890–1976) and Morris Graves (1910–2001). His technical mastery of encaustic painting and his unusually independent development as an artist also serve as hallmarks of his career. In *Cobalt Violet Dark,* Goldberg distills the image to flat areas of strongly contrasting colors and values.

ROBERT C. JONES
BORN WEST HARTFORD,
CONNECTICUT, 1930

Carbon Falls, 1979
Oil on canvas
77¾ × 77¾ inches (197.5 × 197.5 cm)

Gift of Francine Seders, 1993.11

Throughout his career, Robert C. Jones has remained an avid proponent of pure abstraction. One important experience was his studies with Hans Hofmann (1880–1966) in 1952. Hofmann was a leading figure in the New York–based abstract expressionist circles and a widely influential teacher and mentor to generations of American artists. Jones's intent is to paint something beautiful, something he has never seen before. Over the decades, his palette and compositions have shifted perceptibly but always remain fresh and lively.

ROBERT MOTHERWELL

BORN ABERDEEN, WASHINGTON,
1915
DIED PROVINCETOWN, MASSACHU-
SETTS, 1991

*Open No. 176 (in Crimson
with Orange and Black
Line)*, 1970

Acrylic on canvas
60 × 72 inches (152.4 × 182.9 cm)

Museum purchase with the aid of
funds from the National Endowment for the Arts, 1971.44

Robert Motherwell was an eloquent advocate for abstract expressionism both through his work and in his writings and lectures. He sought to communicate sophisticated ideas and emotions through strictly formal means such as color, line, and nonrepresentational shapes. This painting is part of Motherwell's *Open* series, which he began working on in 1969 and continued for the rest of his career. The incomplete rectangular forms in these works float on fields of color, suggesting portals into both physical worlds and intellectual or emotional spaces. Inspired by the placement of windows and doors in his studio, the *Open* series explored variations on the entrance to Greek philosopher Plato's cave and the implications of the Platonic ideal.

JACOB LAWRENCE
BORN ATLANTIC CITY, NEW JERSEY,
1917
DIED SEATTLE, WASHINGTON, 2000

Street Orator's Audience,
1936
Tempera on paper
24 × 19⅛ inches (61 × 48.6 cm)

Gift of Mr. and Mrs. Roger W. Peck
by exchange, 1995.10

Jacob Lawrence was an impassioned observer and storyteller whose art documented both the African American experience as well as the larger human struggle for freedom and social justice. He was raised in Harlem, and his works from the 1930s and 1940s capture the ever-changing street life in gouache, watercolor, and tempera. *Street Orator's Audience* exhibits several characteristic elements of Lawrence's work. Rather than focusing on detail, he chose to use broad, flat areas of color to create his figures and shapes. Further, to better create an interesting narrative, he selected an unusual viewpoint for his scene, recording the crowd's reaction rather than the orator in action.

JACOB LAWRENCE

Brooklyn Stoop, 1967
Gouache and casein on paper
21⅛ × 16⅛ inches (53.7 × 41 cm)

Museum purchase, 1990.7

Ten Builders, 1996
Soft ground etching with aquatint
10¾ × 16¾ inches (27.3 × 42.5 cm)

Partial gift of Marcia Bartholme, Beta Press
and partial Museum purchase, 2001.41.59

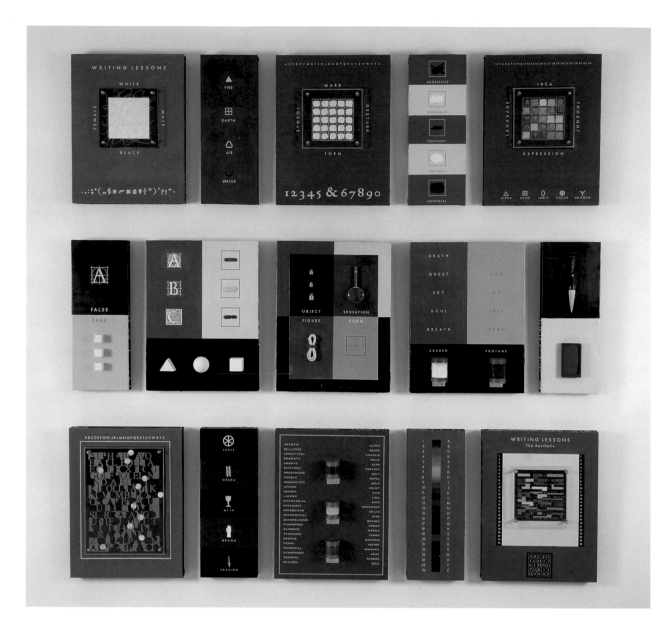

DENNIS EVANS
BORN YAKIMA, WASHINGTON, 1946

Writing Lessons, 2002
Mixed media and encaustic on
canvas on board
15 panels, installed: 84 × 84 inches
(213.4 × 213.4 cm)

Gift of the artist and Woodside-
Braseth Gallery, 2003.34 A-O

Dennis Evans juxtaposes multiple objects with text to represent the complex relationships between language, communication, and art. His deep understanding and passion for linguistics, philosophy, art history, and theology help him to distill core theories into visual forms. By creating a series of equivalent relationships, or contrasting pairs of symbols, Evans declares that there are simple rules for knowledge and communication. In *Writing Lessons* Evans assembles a variety of vocabularies—letters, numbers, colors, shapes—inviting the viewer to join him in shaping them into visual and literal messages.

DENNIS EVANS

The Bridge to
  Caduceatores, 1980s
Mixed media on paper
38 × 76 inches (96.5 × 193 cm)

Gift of the Bell Family Collection,
2008.16

Box for Instruments
  (Shrine 7), 1979
Wood, lacquer, porcelain, brass,
string, wax, and copper
22½ × 17¼ × 8¾ inches
(57.2 × 43.8 × 22.2 cm)

Gift of Lannan Foundation,
1999.38.3 A-HH

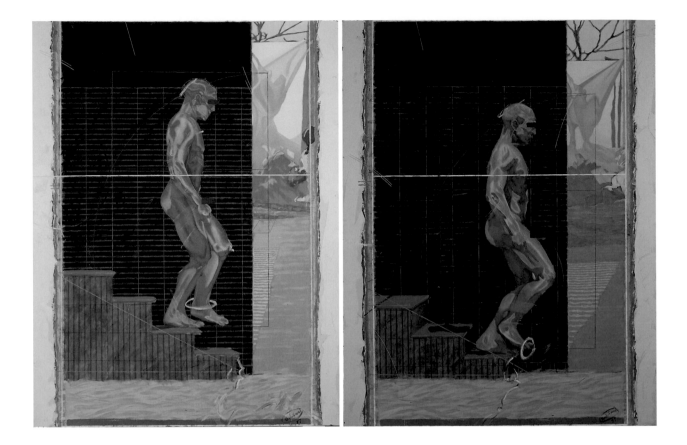

JAY BACKSTRAND
BORN SALEM, OREGON, 1934

Stepping Down 1 & 2,
 1977
Oil, wax, and mixed media on
canvas
Two panels, installed: 78 × 120 inches
(198.1 × 304.8 cm)

Gift of George H. Fleerlage in
memory of Harvey D. Horne, MD,
2008.11 A-B

Jay Backstrand developed his signature style of figuration and appropriation during his
studies in London in the mid-1960s, at which time he had access to works by leading contemporary artists, including R. B. Kitaj (1932–2007). Central to Backstrand's artistic practice
has been his insistence that his paintings are simply formal compositions that have meaning only when considered by an informed viewer, who brings his or her experiences and
knowledge to the works. This composition is reminiscent of the photographs of the motion-
study artist Eadweard Muybridge (1830–1904) as well as Marcel Duchamp's (1887–1968)
famous *Nude Descending a Staircase (No. 2). Stepping Down 1 & 2* is also significant in the
artist's career as the final work Backstrand completed using oil paint.

CAMILLE PATHA
BORN SEATTLE, WASHINGTON, 1938

The Conductor, 1975
Acrylic on masonite
47¼ × 47¼ inches (120 × 120 cm)

Gift of the artist, 1976.4

Early in her career, Camille Patha rejected her core training in pure abstraction to favor pictorial imagery deeply indebted to surrealism. In the early 1970s, she embraced the expressive potential of surrealism and created her own style—termed metaphorical realism—to explore social issues, ecology, feminism, and sexuality. Although Patha's work is dreamlike, she departs from surrealism in her intent to confront the conscious realm. Filling her paintings with images intended to stimulate and trigger the viewer's life sources, Patha attempts to bring forth those paradoxes and subtleties that constitute life itself. In *The Conductor,* Patha's meticulous—if seemingly unlikely—selection of images references the multidimensional and expansive aspects of human desire and how we as viewers selectively choose what to show to others.

FRANCIS CELENTANO
BORN BRONX, NEW YORK, 1928

Alternating Curve of Isis,
1981
Acrylic on plastic adhered to panel
15½ × 94 inches (39.4 × 238.8 cm)

Gift of Safeco Insurance, a member of the Liberty Mutual Group, and Washington Art Consortium, 2010.6.22

Francis Celentano is one of the few Northwest practitioners of op art, a form of geometric abstraction that creates and plays with optical illusion. Celentano works not only with pattern but also with intense color, particularly, as in this work, the rainbow spectrum. He also experiments with the shapes and scale of his canvases, ranging from traditional rectangles through a variety of unusual shapes, often distorting or dramatically elongating them. In his works, color and pattern play off of each other to create a dynamic energy and sense of movement and depth.

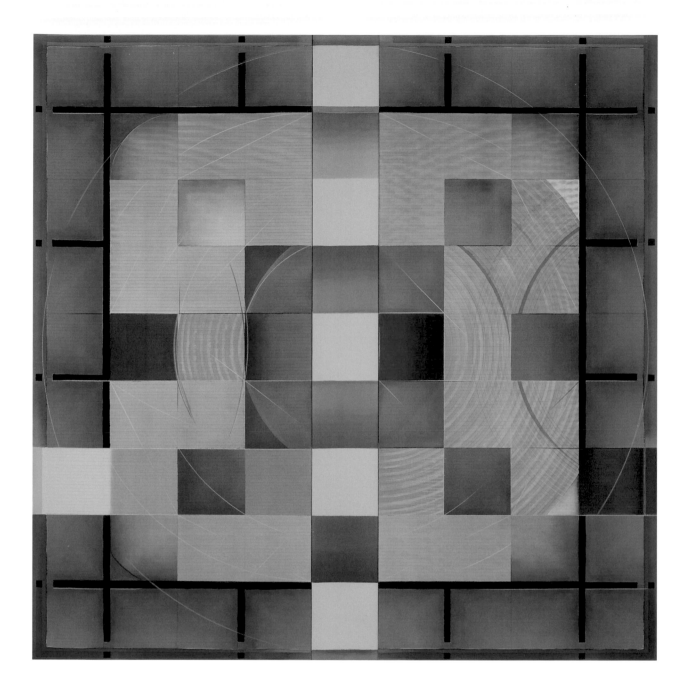

WILLIAM HOPPE
BORN PORTAGE, WASHINGTON, 1945

The Mute Siren, 1981
Acrylic on canvas
Three panels, installed:
94 × 94 inches (238.8 × 238.8 cm)

Gift of Virginia and Bagley Wright,
2010.3

Throughout his career, William Hoppe has worked with the vocabularies of geometry, abstraction, and repetition to create powerful large-scale works that pulse with energy. He also is known for his use of strong, bright colors and eccentric canvas shapes to further extend and activate his designs beyond the edges of the support. His works are most closely identified with the movement known as op art, where color and design are used to create optical illusions and confound the viewer's eye. The title of this work articulates Hoppe's underlying desire to create work that communicates without words: the irresistibly alluring voice of the mythological siren is here replaced by visual seductions.

DALE CHIHULY
BORN TACOMA, WASHINGTON, 1941

Ma Chihuly's Floats,
1992–97, 2009–10
Blown glass
Dimensions variable

Gift of the artist, 2006.13, 2011.9.2, 2011.9.3

Dale Chihuly's glass floats were inspired by the glass net floats he found washed up on the Pacific Ocean beaches his family visited when he was a child. The works are deceptively simple in appearance but require the skill of master glassblowers to create the layers of colored glass and to handle the great weight of the glass required to make them. Tacoma Art Museum's Niijima Floats installation was specifically designed to sit atop the untitled wavelike sculpture by Richard Rhodes (born 1961) in the museum's central courtyard and was given and titled in honor of Chihuly's mother, Viola. *Ma Chihuly's Floats* are part of a retrospective collection of Chihuly's work donated by the artist to the museum in recognition of his Tacoma roots.

Pale Pink and Clear Basket, 1977
Blown glass
7½ inches high × 11 inches diameter (19.1 × 27.9 cm)

Museum purchase with funds from the Jane Palmer
Memorial, 1979.2.1

*Oxblood Soft Cylinder with Payne's
Gray Drawing,* 1984
Blown glass
10½ × 12½ × 10 inches (26.7 × 31.8 × 25.4 cm)

Gift of the artist in honor of his parents, Viola
and George, and his brother, George W. Chihuly,
1990.10.24

DALE CHIHULY

*Tabac Basket Set with
Black Lip Wraps,*
1977-87
Blown glass
Dimensions variable

Gift of the artist in honor of his
parents, Viola and George, and
his brother, George W. Chihuly,
1990.10.29 A-RR

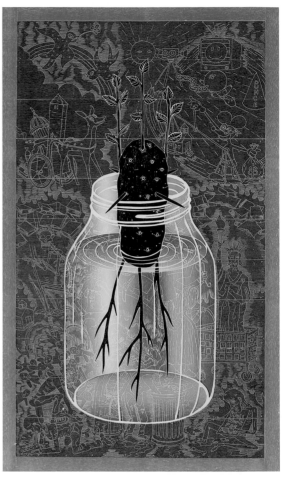

Argosy, 1999
Woodcut
60 × 36 inches (152.4 × 91.4 cm)

Museum purchase, 2001.3

Art © John Buck / Licensed by
VAGA, New York, NY

JOHN BUCK
BORN AMES, IOWA, 1946

Potato, 1998
Blown and lampworked glass
37½ × 10 × 10 inches (95.3 × 25.4 ×
25.4 cm)

Gift of Greg Kucera and
Larry Yocom, 2002.23

Art © John Buck / Licensed by
VAGA, New York, NY

John Buck is best known for his wood sculptures that combine nude figures with heads or elaborate headdresses composed from his complex iconography of symbols, shapes, and natural forms. While an artist in residence at Pilchuck Glass School in 1997 and 1998, Buck learned to blow and lampwork glass. He created a series of works, including *Potato,* reminiscent of childhood experiments starting plants from pieces of potato, plant cuttings, and seeds and observing the growth of their root systems through the transparent sides of glass jars.

JOHN BUCK

Dragon House, 1981
Paint, canvas, wood, and chalk
83½ × 110¾ × 12 inches
(212.1 × 281.3 × 30.5 cm)

Partial gift and purchase from Taco
Bell Corporation, 1999.18.1 A-M

Art © John Buck / Licensed by
VAGA, New York, NY

PAUL BERGER
BORN THE DALLES, OREGON, 1948

Cycloptic #2343, 1978,
printed 1979
Gelatin silver print
6¼ × 12¾ inches (15.9 × 32.4 cm)

Gift of the Bellevue Art Museum,
1998.26.12

Paul Berger began photographing in the 1960s, quickly finding his lifelong interest in arranging sequences of multiple images, sometimes combined with text. Throughout his career, Berger has been fascinated by the relationship between images, text, and meaning. Since the early 1980s, he has worked with digital photography and digital manipulation and has become one of the foremost Northwest practitioners of this photographic technique. With his *Cycloptic* series, Berger made overlapping exposures on 35mm film to create layers of information. Referencing the mythical Cyclops, Berger used his camera's lens to generate an image that combines multiple views and vantage points.

MARSHA BURNS
BORN SEATTLE, WASHINGTON, 1945

Robert, 1985
Gelatin silver print
7¼ × 9 inches (18.4 × 22.9 cm)

Gift of Clinton T. Willour, 2010.4

During the 1980s, Marsha Burns turned her camera to individuals and places on the margins of society. Her photographs captured a generation of unconventional personalities and do-it-yourself fashion trendsetters who sought to create an alternative and safe world for themselves. Made in 1985, *Robert* is from the culminating body of work created in Burns's Seattle studio. These images are studies of existential human struggles, usually focusing on ambiguous sexual themes. This photograph captures the angst of a scream. Separated from the photographer and viewer by the film of plastic, the model's scream is never heard and he is left isolated and helpless.

GAYLEN HANSEN
BORN GARLAND, UTAH, 1921

Kernal Riding through Snakes, 1989
Oil on canvas
60½ × 72 inches (153.7 × 182.9 cm)

Museum purchase and gift of
William and Barbara Street, 1997.32

Gaylen Hansen's paintings are inhabited by a cast of quirky recurring characters seen against loosely painted expressionist backgrounds. The Kernal, the subject of this work, is a lone figure who inhabits the Palouse in eastern Washington. He represents the iconoclastic antihero, celebrated in American culture for the individualism, eccentricities, and heroism required to thrive on the Western frontier. In this painting, the Kernal fearlessly rides through a field of rattlesnakes, almost certainly on his way to another larger-than-life adventure.

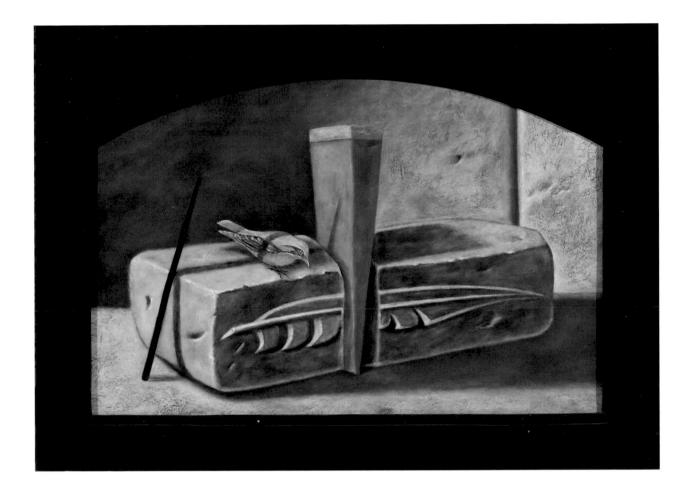

ROBERT HELM
BORN WALLACE, IDAHO, 1943
DIED PULLMAN, WASHINGTON, 2008

Where Birds Go at Night,
1998
Oil on panel
With artist's frame: 29¾ × 42 ×
2⅛ inches (75.6 × 106.7 × 5.4 cm)

Museum purchase and anonymous
gift, 1998.22.1

Robert Helm both painted on and applied wood inlay to wooden panels. He also hand-crafted the heavy wood frames for his works, furthering the illusion of looking through a window into his scenes. His works have an eerie stillness, a sense of stopped time that encourages the viewer to pause and dwell on everyday objects that are often overlooked. He frequently combined objects into enigmatic still lifes that have a dreamlike or surrealist edge. In this work Helm plays on the impossibility of the wooden wedge breaking the stone brick. The perched bird and precariously placed pointer heighten the psychological tension of the composition.

Untitled white with pink sphere, 1981
Blown glass
5 inches high × 8 inches diameter
(12.7 × 20.3 cm)

Gift of Paul Marioni, 2012.8.284

SONJA BLOMDAHL
BORN WALTHAM, MASSACHUSETTS,
1952

Tobak / Red, 1981
Blown glass
5¼ inches high × 9¾ inches
diameter (13.3 × 24.8 cm)

Gift of Safeco Insurance, a member of the Liberty Mutual Group, and Washington Art Consortium, 2010.6.13

Sonja Blomdahl's vessels are based on classical traditional forms, symmetrical in shape with clean, spare lines. A specialist in the *incalmo,* or double bubble, glassblowing technique, she layers different colors of glass to create rich hues that shift in intensity as light moves through them. Her works are a subtle balance of form with color, meant to communicate moods rather than meanings. Blomdahl conveys these messages through her manipulations of color, light, and reflection.

DANTE MARIONI
BORN MILL VALLEY, CALIFORNIA,
1964

Whopper Vases, 1987
Blown glass
Left: 14⅝ × 5¾ inches (37.1 ×
14.6 cm); Right: 23 × 10 inches
(58.4 × 25.4 cm)

Gift of Paul Marioni, 2012.8.207 A-B

Dante Marioni's early interest in glass was sparked by his father Paul Marioni's (born 1941) experiments with glassblowing. Although he was not attracted to the "drip and glob" aesthetic of his father's first works, he became fascinated by the challenges required to master the precision and skill required for traditional Venetian glassblowing techniques. Under the mentorship of renowned glassblowers, including Lino Tagliapietra (born 1934), Marioni has developed a personal style using traditional vessel forms and a highly refined sense of design as the basis for exploring the material possibilities of glass. He is celebrated for his technical precision, the large scale of his vessel forms, and his inspired use of color and transparency.

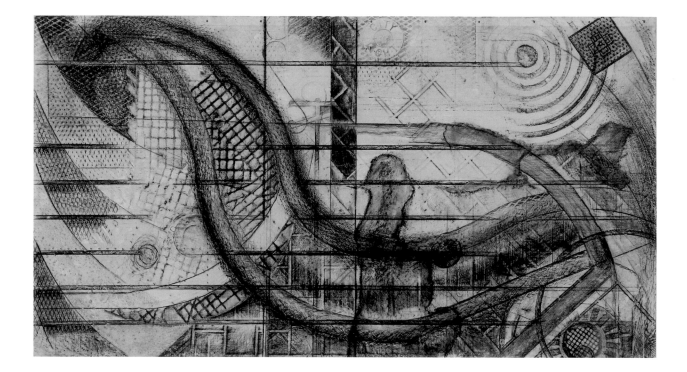

CRIS BRUCH
BORN SUGAR CREEK, MISSOURI, 1957

Main Fourth Washington Third, 1989
Graphite, crayon, and beeswax on paper
44 × 80 inches (111.8 × 203.2 cm)

Transfer from Seattle Arts Commission, 2003.7.1

Cris Bruch's sculptures stem from perfection, patience, and a highly refined aesthetic. Although exact meanings are elusive, Bruch bases his work on rigorous geometry and repetition coupled with time-intensive processes. He also makes his sculptures with a profound sense of social awareness, considering them to be a tribute to working people. Part of his process includes immersion in his environment, experiencing and then re-creating through drawings his street-level understanding of his surroundings. Sometimes, as in this work, he literally captures the streetscape by doing rubbings of architectural elements such as tree grates and manhole covers. These drawings later serve as the basis or inspiration for his sculptures.

JOHN GRADE
BORN MINNEAPOLIS, MINNESOTA, 1970

Between Turf Face and Demesne Wall, 2005
Charcoal on paper
42 × 99 inches (106.7 × 251.5 cm)

Gift of the artist, 2007.35

John Grade made this drawing while he was artist in residence at the Ballinglen Foundation, County Mayo, Ireland. The title is taken from a line in the poem "Bog Queen" by the Irish poet Seamus Heaney. The poet uses the image of an ancient body, preserved in the peat bog, as a metaphor for the endurance and regeneration of Irish nationalism. In Grade's exquisite drawing, the subtle gradations of the charcoal offer a vision of the overwhelming darkness and permanence of the bogs. The reoccurring forms also suggest stones of a so-called demesne wall, an ancient term for a wall defining a property boundary.

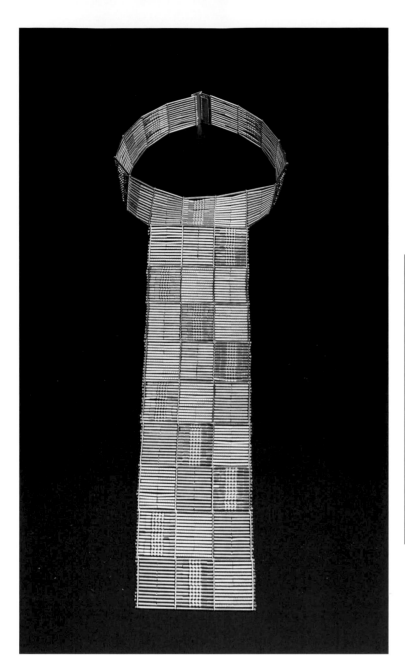

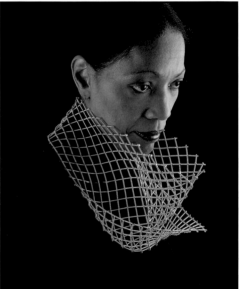

Jayne's Veil, 1996
Silver beads and nylon monofilament
12 × 26 × 12 inches (30.5 × 66 × 30.5 cm)

Gift of the artist in honor of Rock Hushka, 2012.10.6

FLORA BOOK
BORN PERTH AMBOY, NEW JERSEY, 1926

Jayne's Bib, 1998
Silver beads and nylon monofilament
Flat: 16¹/₁₆ × 14 inches (40.8 × 35.6 cm)

Gift of the artist in memory of her daughter Jayne Reitman, 2000.36

Flora Book's jewelry designs are deeply influenced by her roots as a textile designer and her study of the fiber arts. Another key influence was the innovative jewelry made of strands of nylon monofilament created by the English artist Caroline Broadhead (born 1950). Drawn to neutral shades of gray, Book has worked primarily in silver. Since 2000, her work has evolved into other textile processes such as knitting and machine stitching. These works continue her exploration of the contrast between soft and hard while embracing an aesthetic that is more relaxed and expressive.

RAMONA SOLBERG

BORN WATERTOWN, SOUTH DAKOTA, 1921
DIED SEATTLE, WASHINGTON, 2005

Untitled, 1983–84

Paper, glass, Plexiglas, beads, brass, and silver

11 × 6½ × ⅝ inches (27.9 × 16.5 × 1.6 cm)

Gift of the artist, 1999.33.1

The impact of Ramona Solberg's jewelry comes from bold, striking compositions of objects that the artist found uniquely intriguing. Her carefully balanced, often asymmetrical arrangements are testament to her vibrant creativity. Much beloved as a teacher and mentor, Solberg believed that her jewelry should convey a sense of joy. One of Solberg's enduring lessons to her students and the metals community of the Northwest is that "anything goes." By incorporating unexpected and lovely objects into her jewelry, Solberg spotlighted the many ways beauty can be found in the day-to-day world. Although Solberg openly rejected conceptual approaches to jewelry, works such as this untitled necklace demonstrate how she genuinely understood that jewelry strengthens intimate connections between artist and collector. The inclusion of the friendship card was a sincere gesture by Solberg.

MICHAEL BROPHY
BORN PORTLAND, OREGON, 1960

January, 1997
Oil on canvas
78 × 95½ inches (198.1 × 242.6 cm)

Museum purchase from Laura
Russo Gallery with funds from the
Dr. Lester Baskin Memorial Fund,
1998.12

Michael Brophy is often considered the quintessential Northwest artist. His decades-long focus and wry approach to the people, landscape, and history of the region have earned him much attention from collectors, museums, and critics. Although Brophy does not hesitate to depict the difficult realities of a clear-cut mountainside, his paintings also celebrate the regenerative power of nature. In this painting, the exquisite depictions of a rain-soaked logging road and the revitalizing winter rainstorm capture Brophy's fascination with natural forces that also change the landscape. For the artist, images like *January* are calculated to explore pragmatic ideas about the environment. Like many Northwest residents, Brophy believes that logging is a vital industry that provides jobs and raises standards of living through the production of essential forest products. *January* suggests that the costs and benefits of logging practices might be better balanced to benefit forest ecosystems and the Northwest economy.

MICHAEL BROPHY

Small Curtain, 1999
Oil on canvas
48 × 36 inches (121.9 × 91.4 cm)

Gift of Safeco Insurance, a member
of the Liberty Mutual Group, and
Washington Art Consortium, to
Whatcom Museum and Tacoma
Art Museum, 2010.6.15

Sound, 2010
Oil on canvas
54 × 66 inches (137.2 × 167.6 cm)

Gift of Dr. Dale Hall and Susan
Russell Hall in honor of Tacoma Art
Museum's 75th Anniversary, 2012.4

MARK CALDERON
BORN BAKERSFIELD, CALIFORNIA, 1955

Deva, 1992
Sugar palm twine over Styrofoam
37½ × 30 × 30 inches (95.3 × 76.2 × 76.2 cm)

Museum purchase, 1993.9

Mark Calderon draws on a variety of influences in his work, including nature, personal experience, and the aesthetics of Japanese, Mexican, and African cultures. The title of this work, *Deva,* refers to a good spirit or supernatural presence in Buddhism. Calderon's use of palm twine suggests the Buddhist ideals of simplicity and freedom from materialism. The sculpture's shape also references other aspects of the tradition, echoing the forms of temple bells, stupas (shrines), and the topknot of Buddha himself. The work's organic form and rough texture make it seem alive, as if inhabited by the benevolent spirit of the title.

MEL KATZ
BORN BROOKLYN, NEW YORK, 1932

Flagstone, 1987
Vinyl and plastic laminate
on plywood
80½ × 33 × 17½ inches
(204.5 × 83.8 × 44.5 cm)

Gift of Lynn McAllister, 1995.4

Over the course of Mel Katz's career, his work has evolved from abstract painting to shaped canvases before moving off the wall to become three-dimensional works. Because his works move fluidly between drawing, painting, and sculpture, often incorporating elements of all three, Katz prefers to call them "shape paintings." He has used a variety of materials, including industrial substances such as steel, Formica, and fiberglass in addition to the more traditional paint, canvas, wood, and aluminum. He plays with line and shape and the contrast between two and three dimensions as well as displaying a whimsical sense of humor. In a tongue-in-cheek nod to the era in which it was made, *Flagstone* embodies the eclectic design aesthetic of the 1980s, combining a host of patterns, graphic elements, shapes, and textures in a single work.

CHUCK CLOSE
BORN MONROE, WASHINGTON, 1940

Nostalgia #2, 1960
Oil on canvas
46 × 34½ inches (116.8 × 87.6 cm)

Gift of Russell and Marjorie Day,
2005.31.5

Nostalgia #2 is an early painting created while Chuck Close was a student at the University of Washington. Its thickly painted surface, covered with an all-over pattern of geomorphic shapes, is strongly reminiscent of works by the San Francisco Bay–area abstract expressionists, such as Richard Diebenkorn (1922–1993) and Elmer Bischoff (1916–1991). This work is the first painting exhibited by Close. In the late 1960s his work took a dramatic turn away from abstraction when he began to create highly detailed realist portraits based on photographs, the basis for all his later work.

CHUCK CLOSE

Lucas, 1991
Oil on canvas
28 × 24 inches (71.1 × 61 cm)

Promised gift of Jon and
Mary Shirley

BILL COLBY
BORN BELOIT, KANSAS, 1927

Ravine, 1970
Color woodcut
33⅝ × 31½ inches (85.4 × 80 cm)

Gift of the Aloha Club, 1971.21

Bill Colby is a master printmaker with a particular flair for woodcuts. His studies of Japanese woodblock printmaking have informed his own techniques. Colby also regularly experiments with combining printing techniques and other media such as watercolor. His works are inspired by and drawn from nature, particularly those themes that he describes as "powerful yet peaceful." In this image, the landscape elements are abstracted to the point of pure pattern, brought back to the specific by the work's title and the use of the printing block's wood grain to create a surface texture suggestive of rock strata.

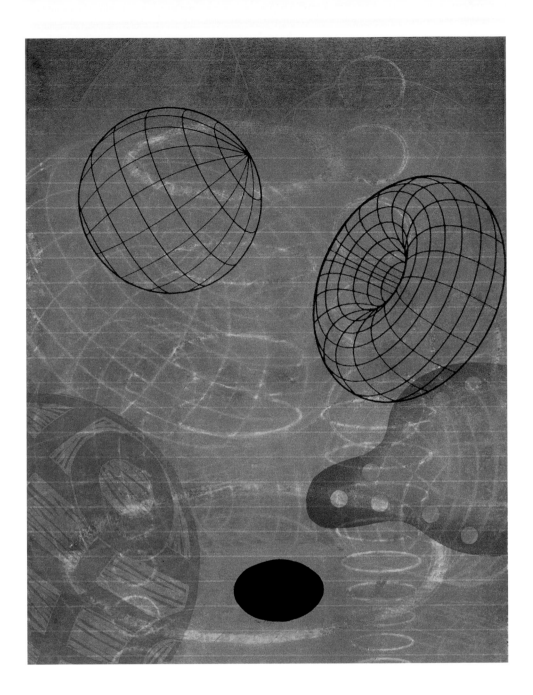

BARBARA ROBERTSON

BORN SPRINGFIELD, MISSOURI, 1952

Ceria 4, 2002

Mixed media and pigment print on
paper, no. 7 from an edition of 10
9⅛ × 7 inches (23.2 × 17.8 cm)

Gift of Safeco Insurance, a member of the Liberty Mutual Group,
and Washington Art Consortium,
2010.6.81

Barbara Robertson creates her prints using a variety of processes as she carefully layers her images. The multiple layers allude to her interest in interdisciplinary studies, namely the relationships between physics, astronomy, and biology. Her motifs emphasize the inter-connectedness between the operating mechanisms of the world from the cellular level to a grand cosmic scale. Using the printing process as a device to create visual density in her compositions, Robertson depicts the geometries of black holes, the spherical form of planets or atomic particles, the storm systems on Jupiter, and the diffusion of energy.

Old Time Picture I, 1999
Mixed media on handmade paper
63 × 51 inches (160 × 129.5 cm)

Gift of the artist and
Charles Froelick, 2001.13

RICK BARTOW
TRIBAL AFFILIATION: WIYOT
BORN NEWPORT, OREGON, 1946

*A Mask for My Brother's
Worry,* 1989
Copper, aluminum, brass, leather,
cedar, and dried grass
53 × 13 × 4½ inches (134.6 × 33 ×
11.4 cm)

Gift of Kathy and Bill Garrett,
2000.27

Rick Bartow draws inspiration for his work from his Native American heritage—specifically transformation stories—as well as from other cultural and personal experiences. Animals, particularly birds, are popular subjects. Bartow works in a variety of media, from drawing and painting to printmaking and sculpture. *A Mask for My Brother's Worry* was made to reveal rather than conceal. Its rough-hewn hammered copper surface and mismatched features made from scraps of metal and leather straps make manifest the worry referenced in the title. Rather than hiding and transforming its wearer's identity like traditional masks, it instead displays the person's deepest emotions and fears.

RANDY HAYES
BORN JACKSON, MISSISSIPPI, 1944

Dying Light in Venice #1,
1986
Pastel on paper under Plexiglas
cutout
Three parts, installed:
79 × 108 inches (200.7 × 274.3 cm)

Gift of Lyn and Gerald Grinstein,
2009.13 A-C

This work is part of a series of paintings and pastels that Randy Hayes created in the early 1980s. He was fascinated by the lives of people he defined as outside the mainstream. He originally focused the series on boxers but then began including others he saw on the street, such as the skaters in this work. *Dying Light in Venice #1* is part of a series of drawings that Hayes made from photographs he took of the colorful characters who lived and played on the beaches of Venice, California. In this triptych, Hayes captures the smooth movement of a roller skater, who is lost in the joy of the moment. Hayes's electric palette recalls the energy and spirit of the late 1980s' music and graphic design.

RANDY HAYES

The Ferry to Eagle Lake,
2003
Oil on photographs and pushpins
88 photographs, installed:
64 × 121 inches (162.6 × 307.3 cm)

Gift of the artist in honor of Bill
and Bobby Street, 2003.51 A-JJJJ

CLAIRE COWIE
BORN CHARLOTTE, NORTH
CAROLINA, 1975

Villager XI (Two Trees),
2005
Watercolor on paper
104 × 52 inches (264.2 × 132.1 cm)

Museum purchase with funds from
Rebecca and Alexander Stewart,
2005.45.1

Claire Cowie's paintings offer a delicate and eerie exploration of human behavior through imaginary characters and worlds. Evoking childhood fables and fairy tales, Cowie's creations are surrogates for people facing uncertainty, fear, and desire. She heightens the psychological fragility and other-worldly qualities of her work through shifts in scale and proportion and through compositions that float within a vast, ambiguous terrain. In this work the villagers race threateningly toward an indeterminate goal, simultaneously purposeful and adrift.

FAY JONES
BORN BOSTON, MASSACHUSETTS,
1936

Body Fires, 1991
Acrylic and collage on paper
Three panels, installed:
79 × 157½ inches (200.7 × 400.1 cm)

Museum purchase, 1992.9 A-C

Fay Jones works primarily on paper, using watercolor, acrylic, and sumi ink as well as collage elements. Over time she has developed a recurring group of characters who appear and reappear in different combinations and relationships. In her earlier works, the backgrounds were often covered with patterns or other detail, but over time she began to focus more intently on the characters. Her works explore interpersonal relationships and question social conventions, often with a wry sense of humor. Here she makes literal some of the common clichés about fire and the body.

JOE FEDDERSEN
TRIBAL AFFILIATION: COLVILLE /
OKANAGAN
BORN OMAK, WASHINGTON, 1953

Rainscape, circa 1983
Silkscreen
Two panels, installed:
44¼ × 67¾ inches
(112.4 × 172.1 cm)

Gift of Mr. Tom Gorman,
1998.53 A-B

Joe Feddersen is a printmaker as well as a glass and textile artist. In the tradition of his Plateau Indian ancestors, he uses symbols in his work to record the landscapes around him, both rural and urban. In Plateau design, geometric motifs on baskets and weavings represent topographical details and other markers of a particular place. Feddersen has created his own symbol system to record details of his contemporary environment, including stylized tire tracks, parking-lot stripes, and utility towers. One of the first prints he created while he was a student at the University of Washington, *Rainscape* refers to both the iconic ukiyo-e print by Utagawa Hiroshige (1797–1858) from the 19th century and the typical Northwest rainy day.

JOE FEDDERSEN

Plateau Geometric #35,
  1996
Monotype
11⅞ × 11⅞ inches (30.2 × 30.2 cm)

Gift of the artist, 1997.1.2

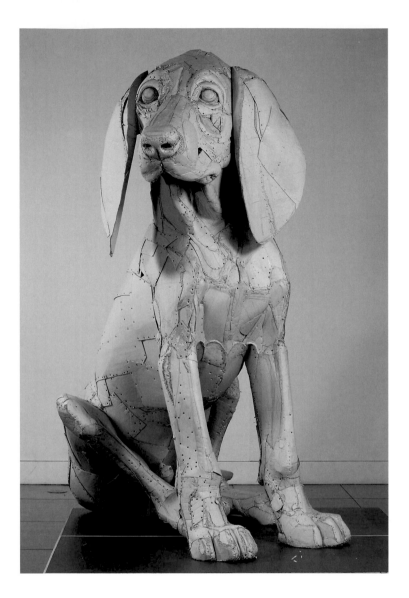

SCOTT FIFE
BORN MOSCOW, IDAHO, 1949

Leroy, The Big Pup, 2004
Archival cardboard, carpenter's
glue, and drywall screws
118 × 54 × 140 inches
(299.7 × 137.2 × 355.6 cm)

Scott Fife follows in the footsteps of pop artists from the 1960s and 1970s by focusing on the fads and fascinations of American culture and using nontraditional materials to create his sculptures. Beginning with commercial products, he turned to objects from everyday life and also created a series of portraits of celebrities, all fashioned using archival cardboard, glue, and screws. To give these simple things greater cachet, Fife often re-creates them at an exaggerated scale, making them literally larger than life. His sculpture of his dog, Leroy, was acquired in 2007 and has since become the museum's mascot.

Acquired with a major contribution from Theodore M. Wight in honor of Minot Rhys Tomala and Madeline Patricia Tomala; and a major contribution from Virginia Davis Wight in honor of her great-grandchildren Minot Rhys Tomala, Madeline Patricia Tomala, Sidney Jordan Evans, Lachlan Hewitt Barnes, Anika Holly Wight, Colby Davis McArthur, Hollis Parks McArthur, and Cassidy Brooke McArthur. Additional donations received from John and Shari Behnke; Corinne Dixon; Gail Elliott in honor of Scooter, Lucy, Rudy, Odie, Sweetie, and Kirin; Paul I. Gingrich Jr.; Tana Givens and Abby Givens; Esther M. Grant and Kristine Grant McLean; The Griffin Family; Todd Heistuman and Susan H. Lambert; Joanne Holderman in honor of Lauren and Grace Holderman; Ann and Robert Lockwood in honor of Robert William and Elizabeth Lockwood; Dan and Pat Nelson; Gary N. Owen; Stephanie A. Stebich in honor of her grandmother Lili Cummings; Bill and Bobby Street in honor of Anna for her love of dogs; Jim and Ann Wiborg; and Leroy's Buddies, 2007.26

SCOTT FIFE

Dresser with Drapes and
*   Landscape,* 1991
Archival cardboard with Lascaux
paint
59 × 47 × 9 inches (149.9 × 119.4 ×
22.9 cm)

Gift of Les J. and Karen Weinstein,
2007.29

CLAUDIA FITCH

BORN PALO ALTO, CALIFORNIA, 1952

Two Chandeliers with Milk Drops, 2003
Ceramic with glazes, oil paint, gold leaf, and brass fittings
Dimensions variable

Museum purchase with funds from Shari and John Behnke and Greg Kucera and Larry Yocom, 2007.28

Claudia Fitch incorporates bold imagery from art that spans centuries and cultures. These symbols sometimes appear in her dreams in unusual roles, and she often is inspired by her seemingly nonsensical dreams to create the work of art. The resulting sculptures convey the surreal order and juxtaposition of things and people that she remembers from her dreams. In *Two Chandeliers with Milk Drops,* she depicts upside-down Buddha-like figures that seep gilded drops of milk. This unearthly scene evokes a serene sense of compassion and a promise of security and prosperity, as symbolized by the milk drops.

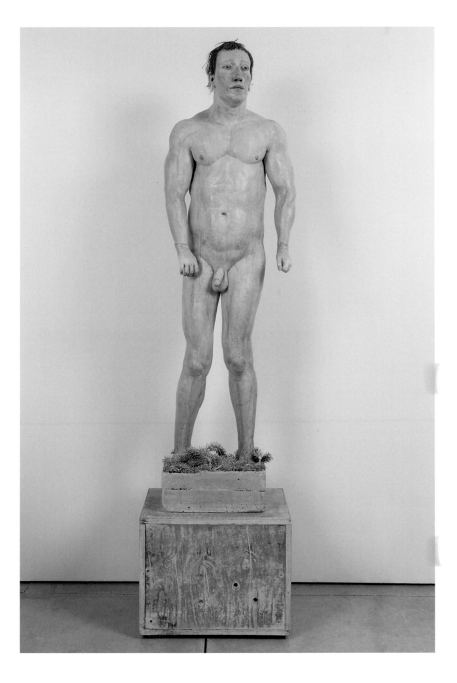

DOUG JECK
BORN JERSEY CITY, NEW JERSEY,
1963

Cain and Abel, 2000
Stoneware, paint, concrete, plastic
foliage, wax, hair, and wood
77 × 20 × 16 inches (195.6 × 50.8 ×
40.6 cm)

Museum purchase with funds from
the Howard Kottler Testamentary
Trust, 2001.16 A-B

Ambiguity is a key component of Doug Jeck's ceramic sculptures. His figures reference classical forms while simultaneously subverting the tradition: they mimic stone but are made of clay; fragments are sometimes missing or recombined to unsettling effect; the inclusion of hair, fabric, and bits of organic material blurs the line between living flesh and its facsimile. Many seem vulnerable, uncertain, even distressed at finding themselves thrust forward into the public eye. Jeck has described his figures as remnants of the heroicized past confronting and often confounded by the complexities of the antiheroic present. The sculpture *Cain and Abel* references the biblical tale of the two sons of Adam and Eve. Instead of recalling the conflict between the brothers, Jeck focuses on the relationship between the father and his sons. In this sculpture, which is a self-portrait of sorts, Jeck replaces the adult hands of the father figure with casts of his own son's hands.

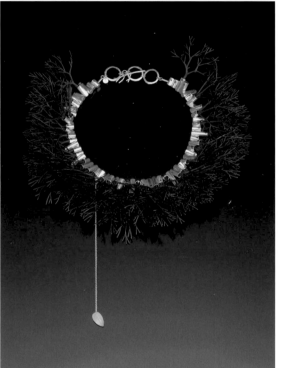

Tree Ruff, 2008
Sterling silver, plastic model railroad tree armatures, and 24-karat gold
12 × 12 × 3 inches (30.5 × 30.5 × 7.6 cm)

Museum purchase in honor of Sharon Campbell from her friends at Rotasa Foundation, 2009.4.4

SARAH HOOD
BORN SEATTLE, WASHINGTON, 1968

Malden Avenue East,
1999
Sterling silver and Chinese lantern pods
8 × 8 × 1 inches (20.3 × 20.3 × 2.5 cm)

Gift of Donna and Ralph Briskin, 2007.34

Sarah Hood's jewelry combines traditional jewelry-making materials with everyday objects, from doll arms to leaves. Her art examines the natural world, its shapes and designs. *Malden Avenue East* is part of her *Decomposition* series that explores the transient nature of organic material and the delights and risks of building objects from fragile natural substances. The resulting works are elegant paradoxes—solid and ephemeral, structured and in flux. *Tree Ruff* is part of a later series that replaces natural materials with plastic replicas, exploring the tension between real and artificial.

LORI TALCOTT
BORN OLYMPIA, WASHINGTON, 1959

Pod Necklace, 1999
Silver and pearls
6 × 6 × 2½ inches (15.2 × 15.2 ×
6.4 cm)

Anonymous gift, 2003.12

Lori Talcott creates jewelry informed by her studies of Scandinavian folk art and ornament as well as medieval designs. Fascinated by the symbolism and meanings woven into
these works, she often references mythological stories, personal events, or the histories of
those who commission her creations. Talcott works primarily with silver, using traditional
techniques of hammering, cutting, and engraving. In some works, like *Pod Necklace,*
she strongly invokes classic designs, but in others she uses her historical knowledge and
methods as a starting point for distinctly contemporary forms.

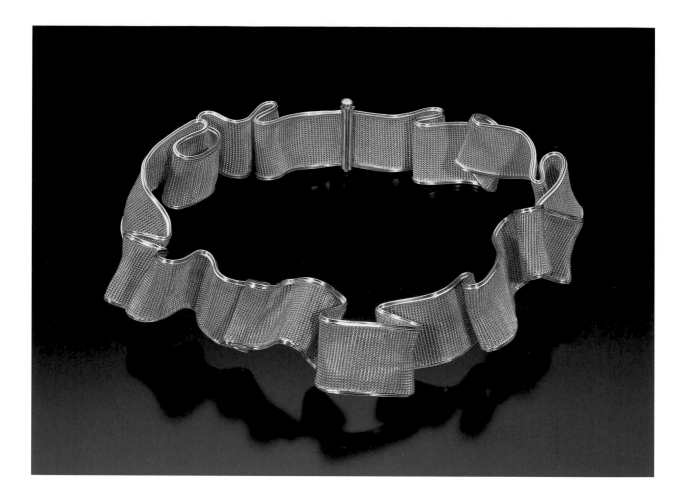

MARY LEE HU
BORN LAKEWOOD, OHIO, 1943

Choker #83, 2000
22-karat and 18-karat gold
6⅛ × 6¼ × 1 inches (15.6 × 15.9 × 2.5 cm)

Mary Lee Hu's works are based on the symmetry and fluidity of natural forms and her works are prized by collectors worldwide for their elegance and masterful, evocative designs. In *Choker #83* she has twisted and woven thin gold wire to evoke two types of body adornment, both a traditional necklace and an undulating, frozen ribbon. The abandon with which Hu has used pure gold to create the flowing lines of her choker reminds us of the metal's rarity and desirability, a substance prized for thousands of years and across all cultures for its beauty and malleability.

Museum purchase with funds from the Rotasa Foundation and Susan Beech with additional contributions from the Art Jewelry Forum, Sharon Campbell, Lloyd E. Herman, Karen Lorene, Mia McEldowney, Mobilia Gallery, Flora Book, Ramona Solberg, Judy Wagonfeld, Nancy Worden, and the Ramona Solberg Endowment, 2006.10

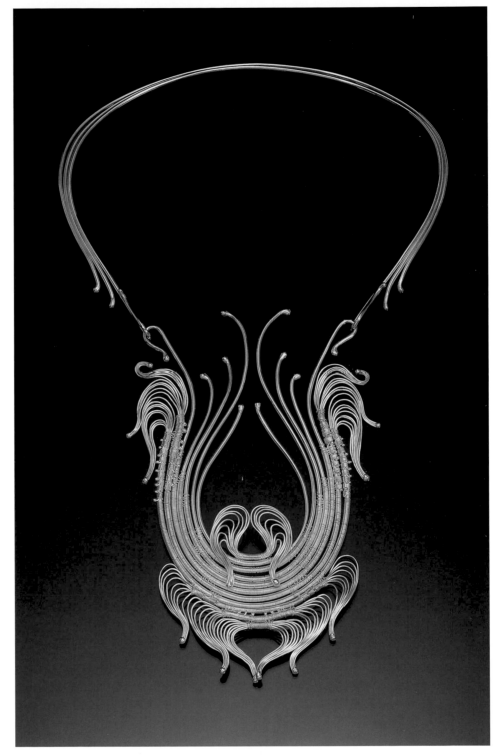

MARY LEE HU

Neckpiece #19, circa 1975
Fine and sterling silver
11¼ × 6½ × ½ inches (28.6 × 16.5 ×
1.3 cm)

Gift of Flora Book, 1998.35.3 A-C

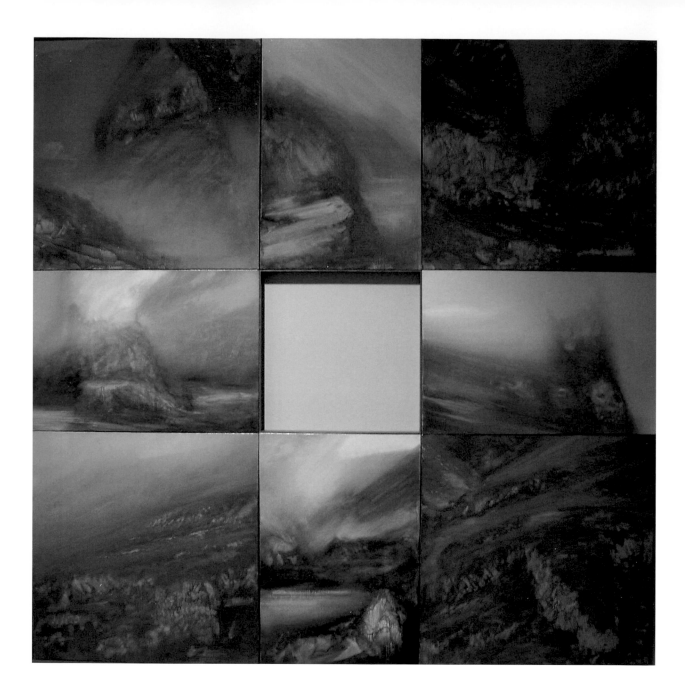

JAMES LAVADOUR
BORN PENDLETON, OREGON, 1951

Release the Sun, 1990–91
Oil on linen
83 × 83 inches (210.8 × 210.8 cm)

Gift of Rebecca and Alexander C.
Stewart, 2000.43.11

James Lavadour grew up around and continues to live on the Umatilla Indian Reservation, outside Pendleton, Oregon. He has said of his work: "I owe everything about my art to the land. It's where I was educated, where I dreamed, got solace and empowerment." Though largely abstract, *Release the Sun* evokes a specific landscape. The shifts in bold color, sweeping paint strokes and smears, and fragmented canvas panels distill the artist's experience in and response to the mountainous terrain of northeastern Oregon. The skull imagery in some of the panels represents the spirits of the artist's ancestors.

JAMES LAVADOUR

Spin, 2010
Oil on panel
60 × 48 inches (152.4 × 121.9 cm)

Promised gift of Lisa Hoffman and
Bill Driscoll in honor of Tacoma Art
Museum's 75th Anniversary

ISAAC LAYMAN
BORN YAKIMA, WASHINGTON, 1977

110%, 2010
Inkjet print, no. 1 from an edition
of 5
12 × 16 inches (30.5 × 40.6 cm)

Gift of Clint Willour, 2010.16.1

Photographer Isaac Layman uses the properties of the latest generation of digital cameras to make what he describes as "hyperreal" photographs. His subjects are all drawn from his home environment. Though the pictures seem like a single shot, they are actually composed of dozens of high-resolution digital images taken from an identical angle and distance and then seamed into a single image using a computer. This image is a composite of 30 digital 4-×-5-inch images taken of the swept-up glass on the kitchen floor after the top shelf of Layman's dishwasher collapsed. *110%* refers to the scale of enlargement of the photograph as well as the imperative for close examination of works of art. This photograph is also part of a group of works that pay homage to the "white writing" paintings of Mark Tobey (1890–1976), which garnered international critical acclaim half a century earlier.

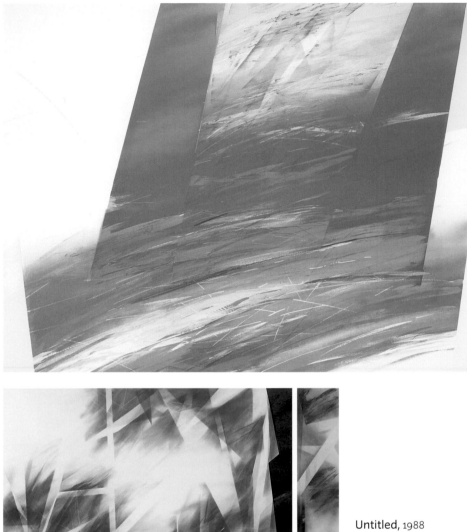

Untitled, 1988
Powdered pigment on paper
Two parts, installed:
38 × 59½ inches (96.5 × 151.1 cm)

Gift of Margaret Levi and
Robert Kaplan, 2005.41.1 A-B

NORIE SATO
BORN SENDAI, MIYAGI PREFECTURE,
JAPAN, 1949

Phosphor Ice Fog, 1986
Lithograph and phosphors on
aluminum
22 × 28 inches (55.9 × 71.1 cm)

Museum purchase, 1989.4

Norie Sato's work is informed by science and natural processes. She is interested in spatial ambiguity and ideas about transparency and opacity, the way light moves through layers of materials, shifts, and transforms. She has experimented with a variety of techniques and media to both inspire and create her works, from traditional printmaking techniques to computer technologies and chemical treatments. *Phosphor Ice Fog* is based on Sato's experimentation with video imagery. By re-creating the visual effects of the minute changes produced by decaying phosphor in a television monitor, Sato captures a singular moment in time. The artist considers these moments of "visual junk" to be reminders of important but often overlooked things, serving as a way to slow the thinking process about fleeting moments.

WILLIAM CUMMING
BORN KALISPELL, MONTANA, 1917
DIED SEATTLE, WASHINGTON, 2010

Kay Gee Doc, 1973
Tempera on board
48 × 52½ inches (121.9 × 133.4 cm)

Gift of JP Morgan Chase, 2009.19.1

William Cumming's works walk the boundary between realism and abstraction. Though he was a figurative painter, his interest was not in photographic detail but rather in recording a moment in time. He was known particularly for his talent at capturing movement: the physical gestures of bodies in motion and the animated spaces between them. He elided or omitted details and often obscured the faces of his figures in some way. The subjects of Cumming's works often reflect his daily life. *Kay Gee Doc* is one of a number of Western-themed images painted while he was living in a rural area and raising horses.

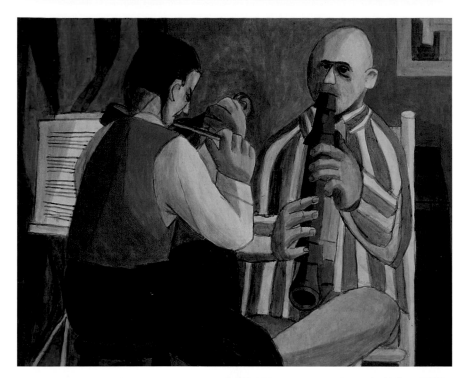

Two Musicians, 1978
Egg tempera on panel
20³⁄₁₆ × 26 inches (51.3 × 66 cm)

Gift of Max Moseley and Grendl
Lofkvist Moseley, 1999.46.1

Kiss, 1964
Polymer on canvas
48 × 48 inches (121.9 × 121.9 cm)

Gift of the artist, 1965.2

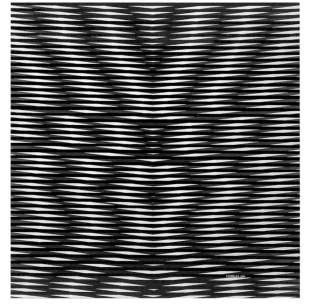

SPENCER MOSELEY
BORN BELLINGHAM, WASHINGTON,
   1925
DIED SEATTLE, WASHINGTON, 1998

All Electric Kitchen, 1949
Oil on canvas
16¹⁄₁₆ × 16 inches (40.8 × 40.6 cm)

Gift of Max Moseley and Grendl
Lofkvist Moseley, 1999.46.2

As a teacher, working artist, and arts advocate, Spencer Moseley was intimately aware of the rapidly changing art world of the 20th century. He treated the numerous shifting styles at midcentury as a vocabulary he could use interchangeably as the mood took him. His works embraced modernism, abstraction, cubism, pop and op art, and a number of other variations throughout his career. Common to all his works were bold color and strong outlines: objects and shapes in his paintings often have an almost three-dimensional impact. In this group of paintings he ranges from the reductive but expressive forms of modernist figuration to the black lines and primary colors of neo-plasticism to the eye-popping dynamism of op art.

PAUL MARIONI
BORN CINCINNATI, OHIO, 1941

*Two Masks: Courage and
Anonymity,* 2001
Blown glass and enamel
Vessel: 19 × 8 × 8¼ inches (48.3 ×
20.3 × 21 cm); Image: 25½ ×
23 inches (64.8 × 58.4 cm)

Museum purchase with funds from
Jon and Mary Shirley, Cathy and
Michael Casteel, Henry T. Schatz,
Dr. Dale Hall and Susan Russell
Hall, Corinne Dixon, Mark and
Nancy Haley, Meri Arnett-Kremian,
and Paul I. Gingrich Jr., 2012.9.1 A-B

After a stint as a filmmaker in the late 1960s, Paul Marioni began to focus on the expressive possibilities of glass in about 1970. In 1974 he developed an ingenious method to create detailed images on molten glass. He continued to refine the technique and was awarded a patent for his process in 1977. *Two Masks: Courage and Anonymity* expresses the artist's admiration for the traditions and independent spirit of Mexico. The ancient culture is represented by the jaguar figure, while the struggles and complexity of contemporary Mexico are distilled into the portrait of Zapatista leader Subcomandante Marcos. Although separated by centuries, these two iconic symbols display courage, strength, and resilience—values cherished by Marioni.

PAUL MARIONI

Prototypes for the Bag
 Man, late 1980s
Blown glass
Left to right: 11¾ × 8½ × 6 inches
(29.8 × 21.6 × 15.2 cm); 11½ ×
7½ × 8¼ inches (29.2 × 19.1 ×
21 cm); 9⅛ × 7¼ × 8½ inches
(23.2 × 18.4 × 21.6 cm)

Gift of Paul Marioni, 2012.8.10 A-C

All it Takes (Nerve), 1973,
 remade 2012
Glass
17¼ × 20¼ inches (43.8 × 51.4 cm)

Museum purchase with funds from
Jon and Mary Shirley, Cathy and
Michael Casteel, Henry T. Schatz,
Dr. Dale Hall and Susan Russell Hall,
Corinne Dixon, Mark and Nancy
Haley, Meri Arnett-Kremian, and
Paul I. Gingrich, Jr., 2012.9.2

Medicine Ball, 1995
Glass beads, papier-mâché, and mixed media
14 × 15 × 13 inches (35.6 × 38.1 × 33 cm)

Gift of Anne Gould Hauberg, 2005.19

Eternal Vigilance, 1983
Papier-mâché, beads, oil paint, sequins, acrylic paint, and fiberglass
60 × 40 × 38 inches (152.4 × 101.6 × 96.5 cm)

Promised gift of William and Barbara Street

SHERRY MARKOVITZ

BORN CHICAGO, ILLINOIS, 1947

Siamese Does, 1980
Oil on linen, beads, and sequins
31½ × 47 inches (80 × 119.4 cm)

Gift of Safeco Insurance, a member of the Liberty Mutual Group, and Washington Art Consortium, 2010.6.68

Sherry Markovitz's works include paintings, sculpture, and images that combine elements of both. Animals, both domestic and wild, and dolls are recurring motifs, representing at various times loss, love, comfort, and security. Her longtime interest in ethnic, tribal, and folk arts is expressed through her naïve painting style and the application of various decorative elements to her sculptures and paintings, including beads, sequins, lace, feathers, and other small objects. Inherent at all levels of her work is the idea of transformation: two-dimensional to three-dimensional, unadorned to decorated, wild to domestic, loss to acceptance.

JOSEPH PARK
BORN OTTAWA, ONTARIO, CANADA,
1964

Chess, 2001
Oil on canvas
20 × 24⅛ inches (50.8 × 61.3 cm)

Gift of David Lewis in honor of
Clinton Williams, Donald Williams,
Eileen Lewis, and Jane Ramm,
2003.73.1

Joseph Park's monochromatic paintings combine multiple visual traditions, including early cinema, Asian animation styles, graphic novels, and pop art. The contrast between absurdity and seriousness is a tool that Park uses to highlight seemingly insignificant aspects of daily life. In this work, the two anthropomorphized rabbits carefully ponder strategy in a friendly game that, despite the title, resembles the ancient game called go, which is extremely popular in east Asia and increasingly so in the United States. The game revolves around the control and capture of the board by moving pieces on a grid system.

*The Ghosts of
Manhattan,* 1982
Sandblasted glass
18¾ × 4½ × 7 inches (47.6 × 11.4 ×
17.8 cm)

Gift of Safeco Insurance, a member of the Liberty Mutual Group,
and Washington Art Consortium,
2010.6.62 A-B

WALTER LIEBERMAN
BORN NEW YORK, NEW YORK, 1954

Aurora Beuys, 2001
Blown glass and enamel
22 × 15 × 6 inches (55.9 × 38.1 ×
15.2 cm)

Gift of Paul Marioni, 2012.8.8

Walter Lieberman has refined the practice of painting on glass, using thin layers of enamel
that are then bound to the object by firing. The process allows for the buildup of numerous thin layers of rich color, lending depth and dimension to his compositions. Lieberman
considers his works manifestations of his ideas, the end products of his experimental, meditative process rather than the goal of his creative endeavors. *Aurora Beuys* memorializes
the performance and installation artist Joseph Beuys (1921–1986), who used his physical
presence and actions as his artistic medium for expressing his themes, an inspiration for
Lieberman's own works.

CAPPY THOMPSON
BORN ALEXANDRIA, VIRGINIA, 1952

Napping Devil, 1987
Painted, stained glass
15¼ × 11¼ inches (38.7 × 28.6 cm)

Gift of Paul Marioni, 2012.8.114

Cappy Thompson first began working with glass when she assisted in a small glass studio in Olympia, Washington. When she moved back to Seattle in the early 1980s, she was invited to begin teaching and creating work at Pilchuck Glass School in Stanwood. There she became interested in techniques for painting stained-glass windows and glass vessels and began making works she calls "picture poems." Her figures and stories are drawn from mythology and folk traditions as well as her own imagination. The image in this work resembles depictions of the devil in medieval illuminated manuscripts, one of her primary sources for inspiration.

ALDEN MASON
BORN EVERETT, WASHINGTON, 1919

Seed Shaker from the
Burpee series, 1975
Oil on canvas
70 × 80 inches (177.8 × 203.2 cm)

Gift of JP Morgan Chase, 2009.19.3

Alden Mason has worked with a variety of media, moving from oil to acrylic and then into watercolor and oil stick. His images have followed a trajectory from abstract to figurative and back again. He has cited artists such as Arshile Gorky (circa 1902–1948) and Willem de Kooning (1904–1997) as influences. In the early 1970s, Mason began his *Burpee* series, paintings based on his fond recollections of the Burpee seed catalog from his childhood. The brilliant coloring and expansive scale of these paintings redirected Northwest art away from the subtle, muted palette traditionally associated with the region since the early 1950s to large-scale, brilliantly colored abstractions in tune with the contemporary issues explored by color-field painters.

ALDEN MASON

Yellow Winner, 1982
Acrylic on canvas
80 × 80 inches (203.2 × 203.2 cm)

Gift of the Bellevue Art Museum,
1998.26.41

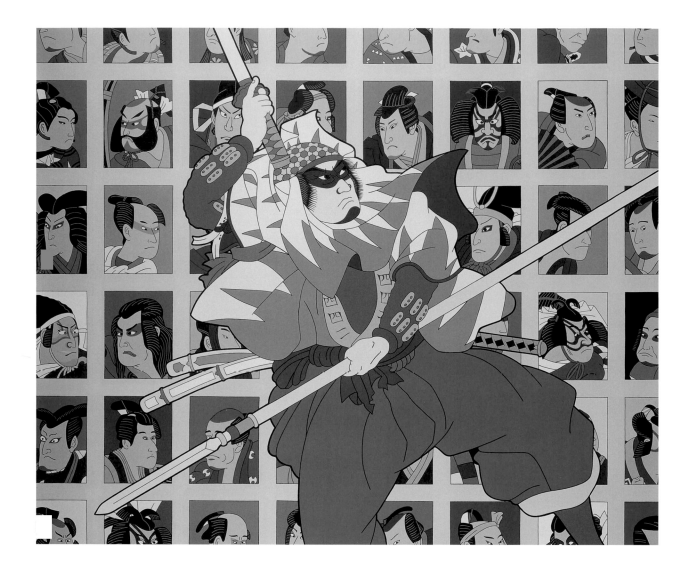

ROGER SHIMOMURA
BORN SEATTLE, WASHINGTON, 1939

Minidoka No. 5 (442nd),
 1979
Acrylic on canvas
58½ × 70½ inches
(148.6 × 179.1 cm)

Gift of George and Kim Suyama,
2003.76

Roger Shimomura was a young child when his family was forced to relocate to the Japanese internment camp at Minidoka, Idaho, in 1942. In 1979 he completed a series of six paintings commemorating his family's experience at the camp. *Minidoka No. 5 (442nd)* honors his uncle, a member of the 442nd Regimental Combat Team, as a samurai warrior with a wounded right arm. Shimomura further acknowledges the bravery and sacrifice of the famed Japanese American battalion by including a grid of portraits in the background, a format that was often used by newspapers during World War II to report the deaths of American soldiers. Each of the soldiers is rendered in the style of Japanese ukiyo-e prints of warrior portraits.

ARNOLD J. KEMP
BORN BOSTON, MASSACHUSETTS,
1968

untitled (Played Twice),
2001
Type c-print mounted on aluminum,
no. 3 from an edition of 7
37 × 31 inches (94 × 78.7 cm)

Gift of Collect 21NW 2011, 2011.8.1

Arnold J. Kemp's *untitled (Played Twice)* is from a series of images he created to rethink the symbolism of the racism and violence associated with the Ku Klux Klan hood. The artist photographed himself wearing hoods sewn from West African cloths. By appropriating a symbol of oppression, Kemp's self-portrait becomes a forceful statement about racial identity and power. The phrase "played twice" alludes to the persistent racism that continually changes its forms—oppression always operates. By wearing the hood, Kemp reclaims the power represented by the hood and morphs it into a symbol of African American resilience.

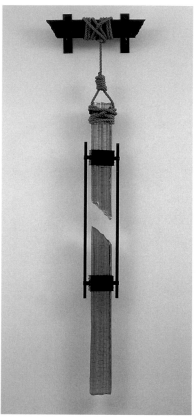

Hanging and Bound Spine from *The Justice Series*, 1997
Glass, steel, and rope
94 × 12 × 4 inches
(238.8 × 30.5 × 10.2 cm)

Gift of the artist and Woodside-Braseth Gallery, 2003.35 A-C

NANCY MEE
BORN SAN FRANCISCO, CALIFORNIA, 1951

Hanging, Healing, 1990
Steel and glass
82⅞ × 46⅞ × 21 inches
(210.5 × 119.1 × 53.3 cm)

Museum purchase, 1990.8 A-E

Nancy Mee's sculptures combine slumped and sandblasted glass with metal, stone, and photographs. She became interested in glass while working at Pilchuck Glass School in the early 1970s. Works such as *Hanging, Healing* explore society's deeply ingrained ideas about beauty and femininity and the profound impact that debilitating diseases such as multiple sclerosis have on a woman's sense of identity. Although glass is a fragile material, by combining it with stone and steel Mee lends her sculptures rugged strength and imposing physical presence. The metaphors of fragility and reinforcement inherent in Mee's sculptures hold a psychological tension that relays the anxiety and fears of women who have been diagnosed with diseases that severely alter a person's body.

KATHRYN GLOWEN
BORN SEATTLE, WASHINGTON, 1941

Dress of Years, 1997
Mixed media
66 × 31 × 7 inches (167.6 × 78.7 × 17.8 cm)

Gift of the artist, 2002.19

Kathryn Glowen is a mixed-media and installation artist whose work explores memory and time. After the death of her friend Mamie L. Rand, Glowen created a series of artworks that tenderly memorialized her. One of these is *Dress of Years,* which marks each of the 101 years of Rand's long, happy, and productive life. Rand was christened in the white cotton dress, and the 101 butterfly tags represent each of the years of her life. Glowen's composition summarizes Rand's personal history, beginning with an infant's garment and accumulating a century of experiences.

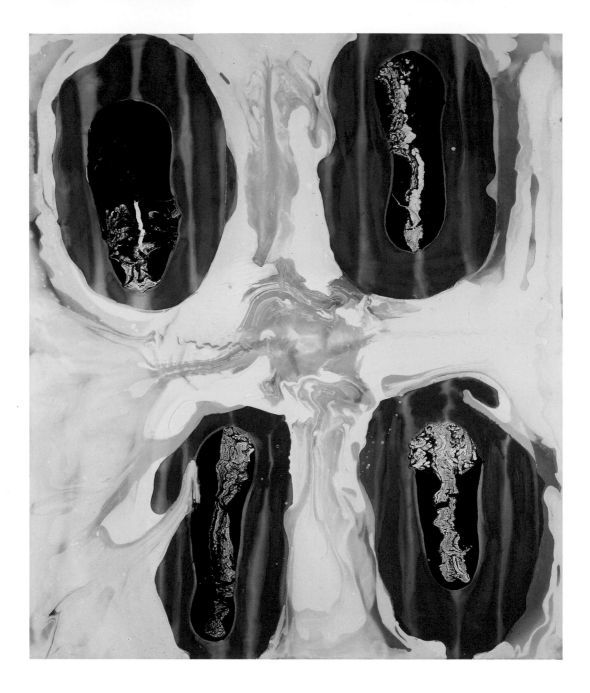

MARK TAKAMICHI MILLER

BORN ENID, OKLAHOMA, 1960

Untitled, 1999
Acrylic on canvas
72 × 64 inches (182.9 × 162.6 cm)

Gift of Ben and Aileen Krohn, 2002.16

Mark Takamichi Miller's large and vibrant canvas is a statement about the act of painting, even though he did not use a single brush to create this work. Miller stained the canvas and poured sticky, gooey paint to build layers of texture and color. The process incorporates chance because the flow of the paint cannot be fully controlled. Miller ensures some degree of control by actually making his own paint, creating liquids that flow and dry exactly as he wants. The result is a unique variety of textures and colors—all focused on the visual impact that creative paint application can yield.

LUCINDA PARKER
BORN BOSTON, MASSACHUSETTS,
1942

Slim Shimmy Shanks,
1984
Acrylic and graphite on canvas
69 × 56 inches (175.3 × 142.2 cm)

Bequest of Kathryn L. Skinner,
2005.42.8

Lucinda Parker uses a fluid, gestural painting style, expressive color, and rich texture to create abstract images full of movement and energy. The abstract shapes she prefers are linear and curvy, almost like writing, rather than hard-edged geometric forms. *Slim Shimmy Shanks* was painted when Parker was beginning to move from painting on the floor toward easel paintings and a more subdued color palette. In this work, and others from this period, she added contrast and detail to her colorful surfaces by spraying powdered graphite on the wet paint.

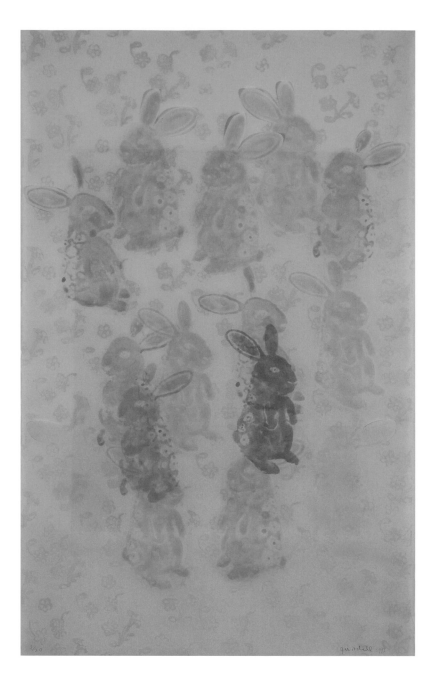

JEFFRY MITCHELL
BORN SEATTLE, WASHINGTON, 1958

Two Rabbits, 1993
Color aquatint and spit bite with
chine collé
38½ × 24½ inches (97.8 × 62.2 cm)

Partial gift of Marcia Bartholme,
Beta Press and partial Museum
purchase, 2001.41.67

Jeffry Mitchell crafts his art with a seemingly casual aesthetic—equally cartoon-like and
funk-inspired—that underscores his understanding of the history of art and contemporary
culture. His style is immediately recognizable, even though he often shifts the aesthetic
emphasis from outrageous and funky to tender, charming, and calming. Mitchell frequently
re-creates his childhood images and emotions in his art. Reoccurring motifs like rabbits,
elephants, stuffed animals, flowers, and religious iconography amplify his attempts to
understand his emotional needs, physical desires, and hopes.

JEFFRY MITCHELL

Hello! Hello!, 2002
Wood, nails, paper, and string
53 × 84 × 41 inches (134.6 × 213.4 ×
104.1 cm)

Gift of Michael Klein in memory of
his parents Hedy and Emil Klein,
2003.2 A-LL

CARL MORRIS

BORN YORBA LINDA, CALIFORNIA,
1911
DIED PORTLAND, OREGON, 1993

Yellow Light Revisited
from the *Intersecting Light* series, 1980
Acrylic on canvas
60 × 90 inches (152.4 × 228.6 cm)

Gift of the Carl and Hilda Morris
Foundation, 1994.3

Over the course of his career, Carl Morris moved from figurative work to full abstraction. His darkly painted realist works gradually gave way to moody abstract paintings informed by nature and poetry and, later, the Northwest's geology. In his *Intersecting Light* series the paintings, like *Yellow Light Revisited,* center on the suggestion of a strong light source from deep within the canvas. This internal light encapsulated Morris's belief that universal qualities may be found in specific subjects. The composition's angular shapes are drawn from his study of geology and further suggest a powerful force emanating from the earth itself.

FRANK OKADA

BORN SEATTLE, WASHINGTON, 1931
DIED EUGENE, OREGON, 2000

Descent I, 1973
Oil on linen
100 × 80 inches (254 × 203.2 cm)

Gift of Robert and Gloria Rogers,
1993.8

Frank Okada's paintings are generally reductive and geometrically structured, deceptively simple studies of color contrasts or monochromatic color fields. He often described his works as dedicatory, meant as offerings to memory, notably that of his parents and the suffering they experienced as a result of their internment during World War II. Other of his works evoked for him locations and moments with personal significance. As well, in their often large scale and focused interest in color, Okada's paintings nod to the influence of abstract expressionism.

HILDA MORRIS
BORN NEW YORK, NEW YORK, 1911
DIED PORTLAND, OREGON, 1991

Myth of the Sea,
circa 1968–70

Bronze
112 × 91 × 51 inches (284.5 × 231.1 × 129.5 cm)

Gift of Wells Fargo Bank, 2001.2

Throughout her distinguished career, Hilda Morris focused on universal themes of human existence and mythology. Best known for monumental bronze sculptures, she also created paintings that evoked the same emotions and energies through abstracted but highly expressive forms. For both her sculpture and paintings, Morris sought inspiration from the aesthetic and formal characteristics of Asian calligraphy. *Myth of the Sea* was displayed in the Pacific National Building in Tacoma for many years before being donated to the museum's collection and has been on view at the Washington State Convention Center, Seattle.

JULIE SPEIDEL
BORN SEATTLE, WASHINGTON, 1941

Malinmore, 1997
Bronze
29 × 24 × 7 inches (73.7 × 61 × 17.8 cm)

Gift of the artist, 1997.17

Julie Speidel grew up in the British Isles fascinated by the prehistoric ruins she saw there, particularly the massive Neolithic stone monuments such as Stonehenge. This early experience proved pivotal to her works, providing the foundation for a symbolic vocabulary that also incorporates influences from a variety of other cultural expressions, including Buddhist art, Northwest Native American imagery, and European modernist sculpture. Working in bronze and stone, Speidel creates sculptures that meld time-honored shapes with a contemporary aesthetic. The compositions and forms of her works are meant to evoke universal meanings, seeking to demonstrate the interconnection of cultures and societies. Malinmore, referenced in the title of this work, is a county in Ireland known for its clusters of megalithic monuments and tombs made from slabs of stone.

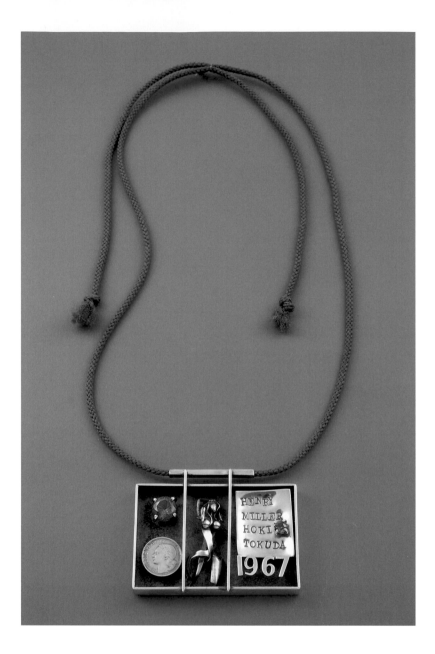

DON TOMPKINS
BORN EVERETT, WASHINGTON, 1933
DIED SEATTLE, WASHINGTON, 1982

Henry Miller,
Hoki Tokuda
(Commemorative
Medal Pendant), 1967
Sterling silver, coin, and
synthetic stones
16½ × 7 × ⅜ inches (41.9 × 17.8 ×
1 cm)

Gift of Russell and Marjorie Day,
2003.52

Though trained in traditional jewelry-making materials and techniques, Don Tompkins began to experiment with materials such as flatware, bottle caps, and other found objects. The resulting works, strongly influenced by both pop and assemblage aesthetics, often convey intense political and satirical agendas. This pendant is from his *Commemorative Medals* series, produced between 1965 and 1976 as symbolic portraits of American icons. It marks the marriage of Henry Miller to Hiroko "Hoki" Tokuda and slyly comments on the celibate arrangements between the older author (ironically made rich and famous for his erotically charged novels) and the young, fashionable nightclub owner.

MICHELE RUSSO
BORN WATERBURY, CONNECTICUT,
1909
DIED PORTLAND, OREGON, 2004

Sacco and Vanzetti, 1994
Acrylic on canvas
43½ × 60 inches (110.5 × 152.4 cm)

Gift of Sally Haley, 1996.6

Michele Russo was a prolific artist committed throughout his career to a reductive figurative style. In his earlier works, his images have a soft, blurry quality that later gives way to hard-edged shapes with bold outlines. Russo used a recurring vocabulary of stylized figures and objects, most often stylishly dressed men, nude women, and accessories such as umbrellas, bowler hats, and shoes. These objects are set against flattened backgrounds composed of neutral fields of color or intersecting geometric planes, suggesting theatrical backdrops or shallow stages rather than particular locations. The two hats in this work are symbolic portraits of Ferdinando Nicola Sacco (1891–1927) and Bartolomeo Vanzetti (1888–1927), who were at the center of one of the 20th century's most notorious criminal cases. Suspected of being part of a secret anarchist group, Sacco and Vanzetti were executed after a series of trials and appeals that were tainted by violations of civil rights owing to overt anti-immigrant and anticommunist biases. Sacco and Vanzetti became folk heroes and were the subject of many works of art as well as plays, books, films, and songs.

WILLIAM MORRIS
BORN CARMEL, CALIFORNIA, 1957

Medicine Jar, 2006
Handblown and sculpted glass
25 × 10 × 10 inches (63.5 × 25.4 × 25.4 cm)

Museum purchase with funds from Anne Gould Hauberg, 2007.6

William Morris draws inspiration for his works from the natural world, ancient cultures, and Native American art and culture. This work was inspired by Egyptian burial objects called canopic jars, vessels that held the internal organs of the deceased after mummification. The lids were surmounted by the animal-shaped heads of the gods of the afterworld. The texture of the jar's surface also suggests the aged and roughened exteriors of long-buried archaeological objects. Morris's re-creation of ancient objects highlights the enduring appeal of glass, using the medium to mimic textures, colors, and forms. The properties of glass, such as fragility and the transmission of light, serve as important metaphors.

WILLIAM MORRIS

Rocks, 1986
Blown glass
4 parts, installed: dimensions
variable

Gift of Safeco Insurance, a member of the Liberty Mutual Group, and Washington Art Consortium, 2010.6.78 A-D

MARVIN OLIVER
TRIBAL AFFILIATION: QUINAULT /
ISLETA-PUEBLO
BORN SEATTLE, WASHINGTON, 1946

Orca, 2002
Watercut, fused, and polished glass
with cast glass inlay and steel base
90 × 64 × 22 inches
(228.6 × 162.6 × 55.9 cm)

Gift of Norma and Leonard
Klorfine, 2009.14

Working in collaboration with expert technicians and the manufacturer Bullseye Glass in Portland, Oregon, Marvin Oliver helped develop a new cutting and fusing process for sheets of colored glass. Using this technique, Oliver transforms the curves and bulges of carved wood into richly colored light that moves through the slumped and fused glass. His work has bridged contemporary art-making practices with traditional Native American themes, stories, and imagery. In *Orca,* Oliver pays homage to the power and mystery of the mighty whale. Through expert manipulation of the quality of light, he emphasizes the spiritual aspects of the totemic orca without losing the commanding physical presence of the monumental wood totems on which the work is modeled.

PRESTON SINGLETARY
TRIBAL AFFILIATION: TLINGIT
BORN SAN FRANCISCO, CALIFORNIA,
1963

Transference, 2005
Blown and sand-carved glass
19 × 16 × 6½ inches (48.3 × 40.6 ×
16.5 cm)

Gift of Anne Gould Hauberg,
2005.11

Preston Singletary's works blend images from his Tlingit heritage with the European modernist glassblowing traditions he learned as an assistant to master glass artists. Singletary uses Native patterns and symbols found traditionally on baskets, wood carvings, and textiles and translates them into glass sculptures that simultaneously reference the forms and innovations of the studio glass movement and the deep historical and cultural roots of Native arts. Many of his sculptures reference specific Tlingit myths and legends. Singletary was one of the first Native artists to work with glass and, through exhibitions, classes, and lectures, has helped inspire other Native artists to work in the medium.

MARY RANDLETT
BORN SEATTLE, WASHINGTON, 1924

Above Paradise,
  Mount Rainier, 1992,
  reprinted 2007
Gelatin silver print
8⅝ × 13⅝ inches (21.9 × 34.6 cm)

Museum purchase with funds from
Nancy S. Nordhoff in honor of Mary
Randlett, 2008.8.20

Mary Randlett is a distinguished landscape and portrait photographer. Her portraits of figures from the Northwest's creative community—poets, novelists, teachers, architects, and
artists—provide invaluable documentation of a time and place, while capturing each sitter's
personality. Over the course of five decades, she has documented more than 500 of the key
figures whose work has defined the Northwest as a region. *Above Paradise, Mount Rainier* is
one of hundreds of images she has taken since the 1940s documenting the unique environment and landscape of the Northwest.

MARY RANDLETT

Mary Randlett, 1988
Gelatin silver print
9¼ × 5³⁄₁₆ inches (23.5 × 13.2 cm)

Gift of the Aloha Club, 2003.31.2

Jacob Lawrence, 1983
Gelatin silver print
10¼ × 11⅜ inches (26 × 28.9 cm)

Gift of the Aloha Club, 2003.31.7

VICTORIA ADAMS
BORN COLUMBUS, OHIO, 1950

Morning Shimmer, 2003
Oil and wax on linen
57¼ × 70 inches (145.4 × 177.8 cm)

Gift of the artist in honor of
Janeanne Upp, courtesy of Winston
Wächter Fine Art, Seattle and New
York, 2003.63

Centuries of landscape painting tradition inform the work of Victoria Adams. Light shimmering through a cloud-laden sky, meandering rivers, and an uninterrupted terrain filled with trees connect this painting to historical artistic conventions. Despite the scene's beauty and serenity, it is eerily empty. Adams deliberately omits any signs of human habitation, editing out roads, farms, and towns. These omissions remind us of how much we value the notion of unspoiled wilderness.

NORMAN LUNDIN
BORN LOS ANGELES, CALIFORNIA,
1938

Simple Still Life No. 2,
1985
Oil on canvas
42⅜ × 66⅛ inches (107.6 × 168 cm)

Gift of American Academy and
Institute of Arts and Letters,
Hassam and Speicher Purchase
Fund, 1987.2.2

Norman Lundin's compositions are spare and dominated by the many shades of gray and muted, characteristically Northwest light. They radiate stillness, oftentimes peaceful but occasionally tense, even ominous, like the works of his often-cited influence Edvard Munch (1863–1944). Lundin's early works included figures but over time have come to focus on simple objects and the spaces around them. He chooses everyday items—a chair, a glass, a jar of paintbrushes—because he does not want the items to dominate the image. Rather he prefers to explore the relationships between form and space and how objects define our perceptions of our environment.

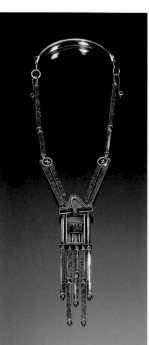

The Shrine, 1993
Silver, charms, ink ribbon, and salvaged typewriter keys and parts
17 × 5 × ½ inches (43.2 × 12.7 × 1.3 cm)

Gift of Rita and Don Newman in honor of Sharon Campbell, 2005.1

Pencil Pie, 1991
Patinated silver, 14 pencil points
2⅜ inches (6 cm), diameter

Gift of Gail M. Brown, 2012.11.6

KIFF SLEMMONS
BORN MAXTON, NORTH CAROLINA, 1944

Leonardo da Vinci from the *Hands of the Heroes* series, circa 1990
Silver
3¼ × 2⅜ × ⁷⁄₁₆ inches (8.3 × 6.7 × 1.1 cm)

Gift of Flora Book, 1998.35.1

Kiff Slemmons makes jewelry that is rich in historical, cultural, and literary references, using symbols to add layers of meaning to her jewelry. She has worked with a variety of materials, from metal and paper to found objects. Her jewelry blends meticulous craft and a handmade aesthetic with elegant, expressive form. Though her concepts and designs are often complex, Slemmons is intrigued by the operation of chance and the ways in which it can transform a finished work. Her body of work reflects her abiding interest in the contrast between the traditional function of jewelry as static ornament and her own explorations of jewelry as a form of personal communication, particularly around issues of feminine identity and personal growth.

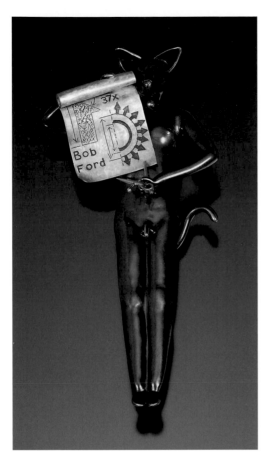

Spit Polish, 1998
Sterling silver
4½ × 2¹⁄₁₆ inches (11.4 × 5.2 cm)

Promised gift of Susan Beech

*Of Rarity Untold (Scene
from an Imaginary
Libretto by Ronald
Firbank),* 1997
Sterling silver, copper, and enamel
on fine silver
2⅜ × 2⅜ × ⅝ inches (6 × 6 × 1.6 cm)

Promised gift of Sharon Campbell

KEITH LEWIS
BORN BELLEFONTE, PENNSYLVANIA,
1959

Our Dear Bob (Pin in
Memory of Bob Ford),
1995
Sterling silver, 14-karat gold plate,
and copper plate
5 × 2½ × 1⅜ inches (12.7 × 6.4 ×
3.5 cm)

Museum purchase with funds from
Sharon Campbell and Phil Baldwin,
2003.79

Jewelry and sculpture are synonymous in the work of Keith Lewis. His objects have a dynamic physical presence that exists independent of the wearer. Through metaphor, allegory, symbols, and wordplay his pins and necklaces speak forcefully about deeply personal issues such as sexual identity and loss or explore the intersections of the personal and political. Though the forms he uses are generally drawn from everyday objects, his works are finely crafted using a variety of metals and enamels resulting in refined and hauntingly distinctive wearable works of art. Lewis earned national critical attention for his work exploring the impact and loss created by the AIDS epidemic and was one of the first Northwest artists to address in depth HIV/AIDS as a critical theme.

MARY HENRY
BORN CALISTOGA, CALIFORNIA, 1913
DIED FREELAND, WHIDBEY ISLAND,
WASHINGTON, 2009

After Scarlatti, 1990
Acrylic on canvas
Three panels, installed:
47¾ × 143¼ inches
(121.3 × 363.9 cm)

Gift of the artist, 1993.1.3 A-C

Mary Henry's body of work mirrors the evolution of modernist ideas in American art in the 20th century. She was primarily interested in the clean, sharp lines and geometry of non-objective abstraction, images constructed solely from shapes and colors rather than derived from a physical object. Her hard-edged compositions, painted in strong colors, are carefully balanced and deceptively simple. In *After Scarlatti* she worked with black, white, and the primary colors to create a work reflective of music by the composer referenced in the title. The individual panels suggest the movements of a symphony and the narrow strips of white and black within the color fields the keys of a piano, while the bright colors and arrangement of shapes suggest the lilting, complex compositions of the baroque composer.

JEFFREY SIMMONS
BORN CINCINNATI, OHIO, 1968

Eulalia, 1998
Oil and alkyd on linen
52½ × 46½ inches (133.4 × 118.1 cm)

Gift of Rebecca and Alexander
Stewart, 1998.24

Jeffrey Simmons's meticulous paintings meld various traditions in abstract painting, from the hard-edged abstractions of early modernists to op art of the 1960s. His primary interest is the optical relationships of carefully chosen color combinations. His art is marked by a technical mastery of diverse painting media and a commitment to rigorous exploration of new permutations of his visual vocabulary. Some of the titles of Simmons's paintings, such as *Eulalia,* were chosen for the feast day of the saint on which the painting was completed. This systematic approach to title selection and the mechanical methods of production are held in dynamic balance by the artist's eye for color and composition.

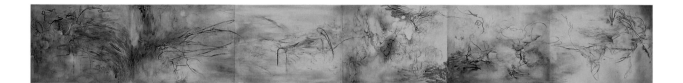

detail

MARY ANN PETERS
BORN BEAUMONT, TEXAS, 1949

*in an instant . . .
    everything,* 2006
Graphite powder, ink, pencil,
watercolor, and gouache on
polypropylene paper
11 × 81¼ inches (27.9 × 206.4 cm)

Museum purchase with funds from
Shari and John Behnke, 2007.22

Mary Ann Peters creates her paintings using a method that has an affinity to the "automatic writing" process developed by surrealist writers. Those early authors and poets attempted to tap directly into the subconscious by allowing themselves to write freely, unbound from logic and grammar. Peters builds each composition from a spontaneous arrangement and accumulation of marks and lines, which are filtered through her aesthetic sense and experience. She uses organic shapes, sinuously curving lines, and washes of graphite and color to build imaginary environments that question our perceptions of perspective and spatial depth. Her images—drawn from sources as diverse as architecture, science, politics, and her personal background—further disorient the viewer by taking familiar details but grouping them in unexpected, sometimes surreal arrangements.

MERRILL WAGNER
BORN SEATTLE, WASHINGTON, 1935

Estuary, 1994
Rustoleum on steel
Two panels, installed:
96 × 96 inches (243.8 × 243.8 cm)

Gift of William Traver Gallery and
the artist, 1997.18 A-B

Merrill Wagner has long been fascinated with the use of nontraditional materials. She has experimented with painting and drawing on stone, steel, and slate, often incorporating the patterns inherent in the material, or marks and blemishes on the surface, into her compositions. For most of her career, she has worked primarily in an abstract vocabulary that has become increasingly minimalist with time. More recently she has begun to study the effects of exposing her raw materials and some finished works to the natural elements, documenting the long-term changes at regular intervals to record the passage of time.

4/200   "Thunderbird"   Qwalsius "Shaun Peterson" 2010

SHAUN PETERSON (QWALSIUS)

TRIBAL AFFILIATION: PUYALLUP
BORN PUYALLUP, WASHINGTON, 1975

Thunderbird, 2010

Inkjet print, no. 3 from an edition
of 200

15 × 13 inches (38.1 × 33 cm)

Gift of the artist, 2010.10

Shaun Peterson's work continues the ancient artistic traditions of the first inhabitants of the Northwest Coast, particularly the many tribes of western Washington and southern British Columbia in Salish territory. He designed *Thunderbird* after the pattern on the apron of the monumental welcome figure in nearby Tollefson Plaza, across Pacific Avenue from Tacoma Art Museum, dedicated on September 18, 2010, by the City of Tacoma. The figure is based on traditional sculptures that were erected near the shoreline to announce that all visitors were welcome. Historically, the site of what is now Tollefson Plaza was the location of an important medicine house and near *spuy'elepebS,* a major village of the Puyallup Tribe. Peterson chose the thunderbird image as a symbol of a lost Native village; the red feathers signify the healing power associated with the thunderbird by the Puyallup Tribe.

**SHAUN PETERSON
(QWALSIUS)**

Welcome Figure
  Maquette, 2003–10
Cedar, steel, graphite, and magnets
29 × 8 × 8 inches (73.7 × 20.3 ×
20.3 cm)

Gift of the artist, 2011.4

ANNE APPLEBY
BORN HARRISBURG, PENNSYLVANIA,
1954

Early Rose, 2005
Oil and wax on canvas
Four panels, installed:
98 × 98 inches (248.9 × 248.9 cm)

Museum purchase with funds from
Rebecca and Alexander Stewart,
2006.2 A-D

Anne Appleby's paintings are minimalist: each canvas glowing with subtle color and arranged with other panels in a grid pattern. Their surfaces are complex and textured, built up with layer upon layer of varied tones. Appleby's works evoke the slow but steady shifts of natural cycles. Each painting traces the seasonal history of a specific plant, here an early rose. She has compared her work to "the time-lapse films in which plants break through the ground," where each small change is documented in slow motion and then combined into a single, fluid transformation.

WHITING TENNIS

BORN EAST HAMPTON, VIRGINIA, 1959

Blue Tarp, 2007

Acrylic and paper collage on canvas
96 × 144 inches (243.8 × 365.8 cm)

Museum purchase in honor of John and Shari Behnke with funds from Edie Adams, Cathy and Michael Casteel, Janet Wright Ketcham, Aileen and Ben Krohn, Greg Kucera and Larry Yocom, Janice Niemi and Dennis Braddock, Grace Nordhoff and Jonathan Beard, Lucy and Herb Pruzan, Carolyn and Kevin Reid, Kim Richter, Laurie and George Schuchart, Rebecca and Alexander Stewart, Virginia and Bagley Wright, 2008.2

The surfaces of Whiting Tennis's works are complex collages of found objects and images, paint and pencil, glue and tape—whatever comes to hand. They often are illusionistic, resembling one material but actually made from another. Tennis's interest in such commonplace materials stems from his understanding of how remote areas, outside of major urban centers, persevere despite suffering natural disasters or long-term economic decline. Tennis originally conceived *Blue Tarp* after noticing the ubiquity of blue tarps in news reporting after Hurricane Katrina and in his travels throughout western Washington. With this conceptual framework that alludes to personal narratives, Tennis approached the creation of *Blue Tarp* from a purely abstract point of view—relating the process of painting to a well-used tarp with faux spills and drops, just like a formal abstract painting. Reflecting on the resilience of the people who use blue tarps for so many different purposes, Tennis similarly explored abstract painting, making gestures that accumulate in a survey of modernist painting, including Barnett Newman (1905–1970), Jackson Pollock (1912–1956), Cy Twombly (1928–2011), Jasper Johns (born 1930), and others.

MICHAEL KENNA
BORN WIDNES, LANCASHIRE,
ENGLAND, 1953

Aoshima Island, Obama,
Honshu, Japan, 2001
Gelatin silver print, no. 6 from an
edition of 45
7⅝ × 7⅝ inches (19.4 × 19.4 cm)

Gift of Clint Willour in honor of
Alison de Lima Greene, 2009.2.1

Photographer Michael Kenna frequently returns to certain locales in order to record them over the course of several years. He has captured the innate beauty in locations as diverse as power plants in central England, the gardens of Versailles, abandoned factories in Detroit, and remote islands in Japan. His signature style evokes a sense of timelessness that underscores the intimate connections of history and geography. This work is from a series of photographs of small islands off the coast of Japan. The images are taken at a distance so as to contemplate the islands' form and geologic essence and exclude the shrines and other man-made structures that inhabit them.

MICHAEL KENNA

Eight Almond Trees,
Casina, Emilia
Romagna, Italy, 2008
Sepia-toned gelatin silver print
7¾ × 7¾ inches (19.7 × 19.7 cm)

Promised gift of Corinne Dixon

Kussharo Lake Tree,
Study 7, Kotan,
Hokkaido, Japan, 2007
Sepia-toned gelatin silver print
7¾ × 7¾ inches (19.7 × 19.7 cm)

Gift of Laura and Sandy Desner,
2009.17

TERRY TOEDTEMEIER
BORN PORTLAND, OREGON, 1947
DIED HOOD RIVER, OREGON, 2008

Untitled, 1978
Gelatin silver print
19½ × 24 inches (49.5 × 61 cm)

Gift of Safeco Insurance, a member of the Liberty Mutual Group, and Washington Art Consortium, 2010.6.90

Terry Toedtemeier's images of the Oregon coastline, desert, and mountains reflect his deep love of the Northwest and his rich understanding of the history of photography. Aesthetically, his starkly beautiful photographs are informed by 19th-century photographers, including Carleton Watkins (1829–1916) and William Henry Jackson (1843–1942). Like these pioneering photographers, Toedtemeier selected his subject matter carefully to create balanced compositions with a rich tonal range. His images of the basalt sea caves and rock formations along Oregon's coast and of the state's stark eastern desert highlands reveal these landscapes' ancient and tortured volcanic histories as well as their rugged, haunting beauty.

TERRY TOEDTEMEIER

*Peter Looking Towards
    the Sea—Cavern on
    North Face of Cape
    Mears, Tillamook Co.,
    Oregon,* 2000
Gelatin silver print
17⅞ × 14¼ inches (45.4 × 36.2 cm)

Gift of the artist, 2002.42.6

Untitled (Hidden History),
    2004
Ultrachrome Inkjet print on Epson
Photo Rag paper
37⅞ × 24 inches (96.2 × 61 cm)

Museum purchase with funds from
the Dr. Lester Baskin Memorial Fund,
2005.28

AKIO TAKAMORI

Actor, 2009
Porcelain with underglaze and
inkjet print
Figure: 16½ × 5 × 4 inches
(41.9 × 12.7 × 10.6 cm)
Photograph: 36 × 24 inches
(91.4 × 60.7 cm)

Promised gift of Herb and
Lucy Pruzan

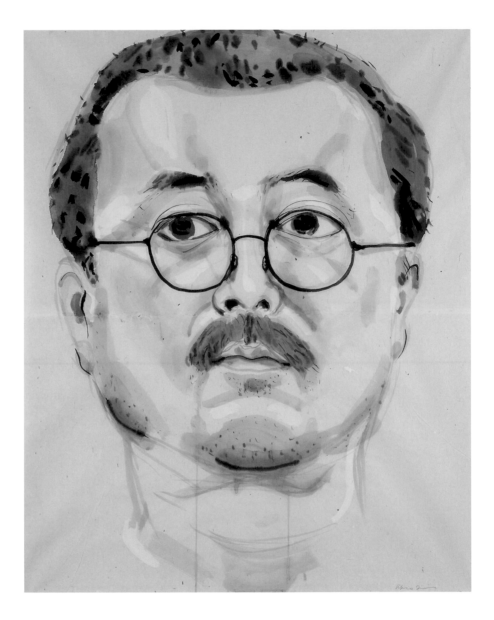

AKIO TAKAMORI
BORN NOBEOKA, MIYAZAKI PREFEC-
TURE, JAPAN, 1950

Self Portrait Drawing,
2002
Handmade Japanese rice paper,
black sumi ink, Japanese watercolors, and white gesso
46¾ × 36 inches (118.7 × 91.4 cm)

Gift of the artist, 2006.18

Akio Takamori is best known for his innovative work in sculptural ceramics. He is one of a group of ceramists at the University of Washington who for several decades have been exploring the possibilities of clay as a medium beyond creating functional objects. Takamori's works are almost exclusively figurative. Many exhibit distinct personalities; he often groups them to create interactions and narratives. Through their forms and relationships he uses his sculptures to explore both public and private personas and how they are shaped by time and culture. In *Self Portrait Drawing* he references his own search for personal and cultural identity.

PATTI WARASHINA
BORN SPOKANE, WASHINGTON, 1940

Achilles' Baptism in the
River Styx, 1996
Ceramic and glazes
64 × 19 × 19 inches (162.6 × 48.3 ×
48.3 cm)

Museum purchase, 2001.38 A-B

Patti Warashina is recognized nationally for her major contributions to the development of ceramic sculpture and her work to redefine the boundaries of sculpture in this medium. Working in clay, and primarily with the human figure, Warashina transforms the medium from a functional substance to an expressive and narrative one. Her art is informed by her role as a woman artist, a working mother, and a sensitive social commentator. She also is known for her wry sense of humor, shown here in this modern and down-to-earth envisioning of the story of the mythical Greek warrior Achilles being dipped in the River Styx as a child to make him immortal. Warashina depicted the magical waters of the river in black, noticeably leaving the heels of the young Achilles unprotected.

PATTI WARASHINA

Amazed, 1984
Porcelain and Plexiglas
57½ × 55⅞ × 6 inches
(146.1 × 141.9 × 15.2 cm)

Gift of the Aloha Club, 1992.11

MARIE WATT
TRIBAL AFFILIATION: SENECA
BORN SEATTLE, WASHINGTON, 1967

Tear This Wall Down,
2007
Reclaimed wool blankets, satin
binding, and thread
61 × 64 inches (154.9 × 162.6 cm)

Museum purchase with funds from
the Aloha Club, 2007.15

Marie Watt is an interdisciplinary artist and social sculptor. A daughter of the Turtle Clan of the Seneca Nation, she draws on indigenous materials, designs, and traditions in her work to address both broad social and personal concerns. *Tear This Wall Down* is related to a series titled *Blanket Stories* that has been installed in six museums across the western United States and at the National Museum of the American Indian–Smithsonian Institution, New York. *Tear This Wall Down* is based on the famous command given by President Ronald Reagan in a 1987 speech at the Brandenburg Gate in Berlin. Watt used the image of a bridge to symbolize the need to reach across ideological barriers between the German Democratic Republic and the Federal Republic of Germany and, more universally, between parts of society separated by other rigid ideologies. The symbolism of bridges has interested Watt since her graduate studies at Yale University, finding resonance between the cellular structure of corn husks and brick construction. Watt developed the bridge imagery in the monumental sculpture *Pedestrian* (2001–2) for the collection of Portland Community College, Sylvania Campus, in Oregon, and *Tear This Wall Down* followed five years later.

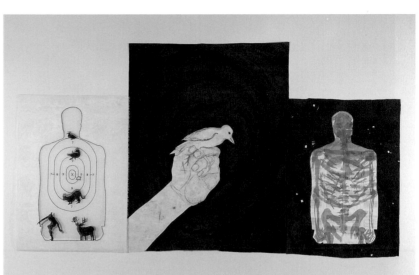

Learning to Discern, 1998
Mixed media on canvas with
reconstructed book and bullet holes
Three panels, installed:
67¼ × 124 inches (170.8 × 315 cm)

Gift of the artist, 2002.31 A-C

LAYNE GOLDSMITH
BORN LONG BEACH, CALIFORNIA,
1950

Blackout, circa 1986
Wool felt
72 × 33 inches (182.9 × 83.8 cm)

Gift of Safeco Insurance, a member of the Liberty Mutual Group,
and Washington Art Consortium,
2010.6.44

Layne Goldsmith uses fiber to make powerful statements about personal, emotional, and political issues. She earned particular national critical acclaim for her felt constructions in the 1980s. One of Goldsmith's innovations was to adapt felting from a functional cloth into hybrid painting and sculptural constructions. In a series of works that includes *Blackout,* Goldsmith used a tornado-like form to reference chaos and uncertainty. She heightened this sense of turmoil by scattering motifs such as birds and tree limbs across the composition, twisting and turning in a vortex of confusion. This image of ongoing natural destruction encapsulates the confusion and anger of artists like Goldsmith and her generation—part political statement at the end of the Reagan era and part artistic protest against the separation of craft-based media from painting. Her later mixed-media construction *Learning to Discern* explores the costs and satisfactions of controlling or unleashing powerful emotions.

SUSAN SEUBERT
BORN INDIANAPOLIS, INDIANA, 1970

Lewis and Clark State Park from the series *10 Most Popular Places to Dump a Body in the Columbia River Gorge*, 1998
Gelatin silver print, artist's proof from an edition of 10
13½ × 17¼ inches (34.3 × 43.8 cm)

Gift of the artist and Froelick Gallery, Portland, 2003.17

Susan Seubert consistently has explored the psychological impact of violence on society. Her series *10 Most Popular Places to Dump a Body in the Columbia River Gorge* grew out of an assignment for a *Los Angeles Times* story about the Oregon serial murderer Keith Jesperson. While photographing people involved in the case at various murder sites, she was both appalled and fascinated that such beautiful and restful places were also the scenes of horrific crimes. With the assistance of the Multnomah County Sheriff's Department, Seubert researched other murder scenes. The result is a group of photographs that melds 20th-century crime-scene photographs with the artistic grand landscape tradition. Each of Seubert's photographs is paired with the text from the official criminal report. The text accompanying *Lewis and Clark State Park* states, "On 5 September 1983, the body of John Lee Hispher was discovered on a footpath West of Lewis and Clark State Park with his throat cut. He was a transient living in the area at the time. In December of 1985, two subjects were arrested after bragging about killing someone in the area and were subsequently found guilty of murder."

SUSAN ROBB
BORN NEW LONDON, CONNECTICUT

Video documentation of
*Warmth, Giant Black
Toobs, no. 4,* 2007
High-definition DVD
20 minutes

Museum purchase with funds
from Kim Richter and Shari and
John Behnke, 2010.1

Susan Robb's work is a form of sociopolitical art making that addresses issues of environ-
mentalism and sustainability. This video documents one of her more eloquent statements
concerning the unfolding crisis of waste plastics in the world's oceans. Recent studies have
identified the dangers of plastic and chemicals entering the food chain and eventually into
human bodies. Her response was *Warmth, Giant Black Toobs,* a series of installations of
gigantic-scale inflated plastic bags. These tubes rise as the sun heats the air inside them,
gently undulating in the breeze. The effect references the oceanic ecosystem that the
discarded plastics are destroying.

NANCY WORDEN
BORN BOSTON, MASSACHUSETTS,
1954

Frozen Dreams, 2004
Silver, nickel-plated copper, nickel
coins, and acrylic
20 × 13½ × 2 inches (50.8 × 34.3 ×
5.1 cm)

Museum purchase with funds from
Janeanne A. Upp and Dale Meyer
and the Ramona Solberg Endowment, 2010.5 A-B

For more than three decades, Nancy Worden has explored the cultural dynamics that shape contemporary social and political agendas, emphasizing the female experience in the United States. Created as a reminder to women who have deferred their life ambitions, *Frozen Dreams* urges through the playful suggestion of liberation that women retain the ability to reignite and fulfill their dreams. At the work's center are facing high heels, nickel plated to make them appear cold and frozen. Eyeglass lenses cascade over the shoulders, front and back, in a pileup that jangles on the body. The clear, sparkly plastics reference the hopes that remain undiminished, even if they are a bit scuffed. Like earlier works, this neck piece is unabashedly feminine, delightful in its ornate decorations, scale, and the playful sounds that come from the dangling components. The work's bold presence encourages anyone wearing it to break up the ice freezing over their hopes and dreams and to get on with life.

NANCY WORDEN

Broken Trust, 1992
Silver, copper, garnet, malachite,
onyx, glass, and paper money
9 × 8 × ⅝ inches (22.9 × 20.3 ×
1.6 cm)

Gift of the artist, 2003.16

BO BARTLETT

BORN COLUMBUS, GEORGIA, 1955

Brooklyn Crucifixion,
2011
Oil on linen
76 × 76 inches (193 × 193 cm)

Gift of the artist in honor of
Marcus Walker, 2011.10

Contemporary figurative painter Bo Bartlett credits the novel *My Name Is Asher Lev*, by Chaim Potok, as a major influence on his career. The book tells the story of Asher Lev, a deeply spiritual artist who struggled with the tension between art and his faith. *Brooklyn Crucifixion* depicts Asher Lev's decision to accept his gifts as an artist and paint his masterpiece, a crucifixion that symbolizes his mother's torment over his decision to become an artist.

Under the direction of Marcus Walker, artistic and managing director, the Lakewood (Washington) Playhouse produced the West Coast premiere of the play *My Name Is Asher Lev* in the spring of 2011. Bartlett painted portraits of the actors who performed in the Lakewood production in his version of *Brooklyn Crucifixion*. To remember Walker, who died in March 2011, Bartlett donated the painting to Tacoma Art Museum to honor his late friend's contributions to the cultural life of the Northwest.

PAINT THIS CEILING UNTIL IT TOUCHES THE FLOOR BELOW.

PAINT THIS FLOOR UNTIL IT TOUCHES THE CEILING ABOVE.

ALEX SCHWEDER
BORN NEW YORK CITY, NEW YORK,
1970

Instructions for This
Space: Painting, 2007
Vinyl, no. 2 from an edition of 10
Dimensions variable

Gift of the artist and Lawrimore
Project, 2008.6

Alex Schweder's training as an architect prepared him well for his explorations of the relationships of bodies and occupied spaces and the various metaphors of the human body as a porous site. *Instructions for This Space: Painting* prompts the viewer to complete the work, with these instructions in vinyl letters on floor and ceiling: "Paint this floor until it touches the ceiling above" and "Paint this ceiling until it touches the floor below." To help viewers imagine how the void would be filled by a solid mass of paint, the letters are deliberately contrasted: the ceiling letters match the color of the floor and the letters on the floor match the ceiling.

MARK MUMFORD
BORN WILMINGTON, DELAWARE,
1959

No One Can Hear Us,
2004
Ink on paper, mounted on Plexiglas
and aluminum
42 × 24½ inches (106.7 × 62.2 cm)

Gift of Shari and John Behnke,
2009.3.2

Mark Mumford's works combine elements of surrealism, pop, and conceptual art. For Mumford, the theory and ideas behind his works are as important as the physical objects. In *No One Can Hear Us,* the stark contrast of black text on white background and the placement of the words creates an abstract two-dimensional design. Viewers add a performative element to the work through their perceptions and responses to the words themselves. Further, the text functions on several levels, reading alternately as frustration, secrecy, or an inside joke of sorts: literally no sound can be heard from the work. This layering of meaning, perception, and questioning is central to Mumford's artistic practice.

LEO SAUL BERK
BORN BURY SAINT EDMUNDS,
ENGLAND, 1973

Ribbon, 2002
Douglas fir veneer harvested in
the Pacific Northwest of the
United States
Dimensions variable

Museum purchase with funds from
Rebecca and Alexander Stewart,
Kim Richter, Janeanne Upp and
Dale Meyer, Josef Vascovitz, Ben
and Aileen Krohn, and David Lewis,
2006.24

In his work, Leo Saul Berk explores relationships between part and whole, idea and result, and visible and hidden spaces, sometimes using 3D modeling software and other computer programs to create his images. His sculptures and drawings are built on complicated conceptual frameworks that extend beyond and often matter more than their physical forms. Made from a continuous strip of wood veneer, in its shape *Ribbon* evokes the massive size of the tree from which it was harvested but in reality is a thin, fragile form. Both protective outer shell and industrially processed remnant of a living tree, it references the critical and complex history of the Northwest's forests and ongoing changes to the forestry industry. The work is re-created for each installation, continually extending the dialogue.

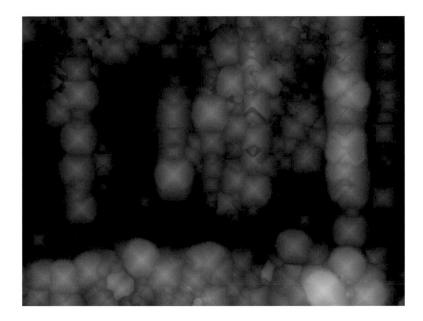

CLAUDE ZERVAS
BORN BELLINGHAM, WASHINGTON,
1963

Forest #3.5, 2005
Digital projection: single-channel
computer algorithm, 4-minute cycle,
continuous digital photograph, Java
program, computer, and projector,
no. 1 from an edition of 1
Dimensions variable

Museum purchase with funds from
Bill and Ruth True, Josef Vascovitz,
and Dawn Zervas, 2005.46

Forest #3.5 is a digital projection based on a single high-resolution digital photograph of a forest clearing in the North Cascade Mountains. Claude Zervas wrote an algorithm to dissolve and reconstitute his digital snapshot. Due to the nature of the mathematical formula, it is a virtual impossibility that a viewer will see the same sequence of pixels twice. The resulting images allude to the beauty and forms of the great stained-glass windows of medieval Europe. This reference ties into the notion of the Western landscape as a "cathedral in the wilderness" that supported the doctrine of westward expansion in the 19th century. By employing advanced computer technology, Zervas emphasizes the shifting relationship between computer technologies and environmental awareness.

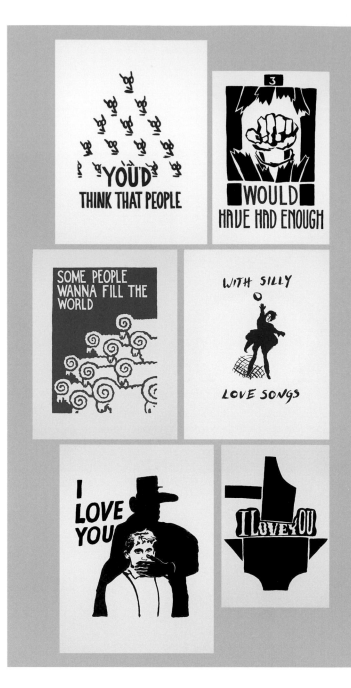

HADLEY + MAXWELL
HADLEY HOWES (BORN TORONTO,
ONTARIO, CANADA, 1973)
MAXWELL STEPHENS (BORN
MONTREAL, QUEBEC, CANADA,
1966)

Silly Love Songs, 2004
Screenprint portfolio
Dimensions variable

Gift of Ben and Aileen Krohn,
2009.11.7.1-14

Hadley + Maxwell is an artistic collaboration between two artists formed in Vancouver, British Columbia, in 1997. They have been working in a variety of media, including video, installation, and sound. This portfolio of 14 prints uses the British American group Wings' 1976 hit "Silly Love Songs" as the basis for compositions that match the breezy pop lyrics with images drawn from student protest posters created by the group Situationist International in the 1960s. The deliberate mismatch between word and image suggests the floating fragments of language and images that surround us in the modern world and from which we strive to create meaning. The artists furthered this disconnect by posting the prints on the streets of Vancouver as signposts to an unidentified and nonexistent event.

JIM HODGES

BORN SPOKANE, WASHINGTON, 1957

Even Here (double blue),
2008

Archival pigment print on Crane portfolio rag paper with varnish overlay

18½ × 14 inches (47 × 35.6 cm)

Gift of Collect 21NW 2011, 2011.8.2

Throughout his distinguished career, Jim Hodges has created works of art that speak to the fragility and preciousness of being alive. Works such as ink drawings of flowers on napkins, an installation of silk scarves, spider webs made from slender silver chain, and mirror mosaics are part of Hodges's expansive vocabulary. He also creates this sense of impermanence in his photographic works. *Even Here (double blue)* is an image of reflected light off the varnished wood floors of a San Francisco gallery. The blue tone evokes the color and nearly unspeakable beauty of the sky on a cloudless day in northern California. Hodges offers structure to the photograph through the central placement of an indistinct window mullion, a kind of reassurance of stability and permanence in the glow of a plane of reflected sunlight.

BILL JACOBSON
BORN NORWICH, CONNECTICUT, 1955

Place (Series) #422, 2010
Pigment print mounted on archival
rag board
30 × 24 inches (76.2 × 61 cm)

Gift of the artist, 2011.7

In 2010 photographer Bill Jacobson was invited to return to the Northwest and explore Tacoma as a subject for aesthetic consideration. Previously best known for his soft-focus images, Jacobson continued his interest in photographs that are simultaneously realistic and abstract. In this work Jacobson seeks to define the relationship between architecture and the construction of space by placing white or black boards in found situations as metaphors for construction. Jacobson said of this work: "I arrived in Tacoma without preconceived ideas as to what I might find. For a week I had the freedom to explore the city and its multiple landscapes. Looking led to discovery, and my subsequent responses led to the images. . . . Though they may appear generic, these pictures could not have been made elsewhere."

MATIKA WILBUR
TRIBAL AFFILIATION: SWINOMISH /
TULALIP

Qwalsius, September 18,
2010
Gelatin silver print
16 × 9¾ inches (40.6 × 24.8 cm)

Gift of Collect 21NW 2011, 2011.8.3

Matika Wilbur is a Tulalip tribal member and was raised on the Swinomish Indian Reservation in Washington State. Her work examines Native peoples' struggles in grappling with cultural duality and defining self-identity in a contemporary world. This image was one of a series of photographs commissioned from Wilbur by Tacoma Art Museum in conjunction with the exhibition *Mighty Tacoma: Photographic Portrait 2010*, a survey of contemporary images of the city on the occasion of the museum's 75th anniversary. Wilbur photographed the ceremony celebrating the installation and dedication of the monumental welcome figure by the Puyallup sculptor Qwalsius (also known as Shaun Peterson), a collaborative project between the City of Tacoma and Tacoma Art Museum. Wilbur captured Qwalsius's expression during the part of the ceremony in which the participants reflected on the artist's family and the legacy he was gifting to future generations.

ALICE WHEELER
BORN KANSAS CITY, MISSOURI, 1961

*Apple Blossom Queen
at the Daffodil Parade,
Tacoma 2003,* 2006
Chromogenic print, no. 1 from
an edition of 3
24 × 19 inches (61 × 48.3 cm)

Museum purchase with funds from
Ben and Aileen Krohn, 2007.50

In her work, Alice Wheeler often seizes upon unexpected juxtapositions. This photo of the Apple Blossom Queen was created by happenstance when Wheeler saw the queen and her court conversing with a soldier while gathering for Tacoma's annual Daffodil Parade, and Wheeler asked them to pose for her. This eye for unusual, even slightly surreal moments is a hallmark of Wheeler's broader body of work, images of both the Northwest and national music scenes. The quirkiness of military personnel juxtaposed with teenage pageant royalty also captures the much-loved independent spirit of Tacoma, where the mixing of different people and communities are expected to build a stronger, more vibrant city.

MATT MCCORMICK
BORN WASHINGTON, DC, 1972

The Great Northwest,
2011–12
Single-channel video, chromira
prints, and ephemera
70 minutes
Dimensions variable

Gift of Collect 21NW 2012,
2012.6 A-H

In *The Great Northwest* Matt McCormick has re-created a 1958 road trip made by four Seattle women. McCormick found their meticulously documented scrapbook in a thrift store and retraced their 3,200-mile route, made in an era before the interstate highway system allowed for simpler travel. During his voyage, McCormick filmed the changes to the places and people that had enchanted the women a half century earlier. His film raises questions about why some things change and adapt while others are abandoned.

VANESSA RENWICK
BORN CHICAGO, ILLINOIS, 1961

Mighty Tacoma, 2011
Single-channel video
Music composed and performed
by Lori Goldston
9 minutes, 11 seconds

Gift of the artist and PDX Contemporary Art, Portland, 2011.5

Vanessa Renwick's works explore ideas about place. *Mighty Tacoma* was commissioned from the artist as part of the Tacoma Art Museum exhibition *Mighty Tacoma: Photographic Portrait 2010.* Renwick frames the powerful mechanical operations of Tacoma's industrial tide flats between the languid waters of Puget Sound and the towering splendor of Mount Rainier. Her film honors the ongoing importance of Tacoma as a port city while continually emphasizing the city's geographical setting. Her deft balancing of the man-made city and the region's natural ecosystems illuminates the range and qualities of beauty that inform day-to-day life in Tacoma. This dichotomy also serves as a gentle but eloquent reminder of the fleeting qualities and miniscule scope of human endeavor.

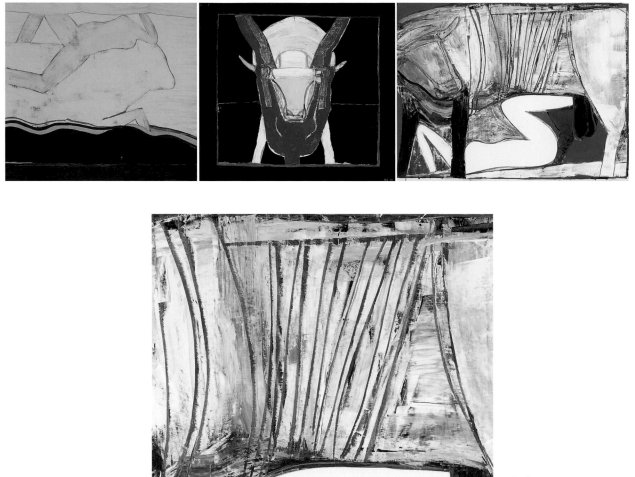

detail

MICHAEL SPAFFORD
BORN PALM SPRINGS, CALIFORNIA,
1935

Europa and the Bull, 1986
Oil paint and cutout on canvas
Three panels, installed:
76 × 249 inches (193 × 632.5 cm)

Gift of Terry Hunziker, 2005.15 A-C

For much of his career, Michael Spafford has used ancient Western mythology and its underlying psychological frameworks as a source for his subjects and symbols that he has expressed through a rigorous vocabulary of modernist painting. This work retells the story of the young Phoenician princess Europa, who attracted the attention of the Greek god Zeus. Disguised as a bull, Zeus kidnapped Europa and spirited her to the island of Crete by swimming across the Mediterranean Sea. Europa bore Zeus three sons, including Minos, the legendary king of ancient Crete. Although it is virtually impossible not to focus on the narrative aspects of the painting, Spafford privileges his works as whole and complete formal arrangements. For the artist, the strength and vigor of his work comes from his meticulous brushwork and dynamic composition of solid forms activated by negative spaces.

Rio Balsas, 1977
Oil on canvas
70 × 46 inches (177.8 × 116.8 cm)

Gift of the Bellevue Art Museum,
1998.26.9

ALFREDO ARREGUÍN
BORN MORELIA, MICHOACAN,
MEXICO, 1935

Frida's Messengers, 1992
Serigraph
24 × 17¼ inches (61 × 43.8 cm)

Gift of Alfredo Arreguín and
Susan Lytle, 1993.2

Alfredo Arreguín is one of the few Northwest artists of the pattern and decoration movement. He has repeatedly used images of the artist Frida Kahlo (1907–1954) in his work, noting that for him she is symbolic of Mexico, where they were both born and trained at the same school. He sees in her a dark side that evokes the mystery and power of the jungle. As in this print, Arreguín often surrounds the central image of Kahlo with dense patterns in brilliant colors that come from a variety of sources, including Mayan and Aztec motifs.

Bird with Nest, 1957
Stone and wood
8 × 14 × 4 inches (20.3 × 35.6 ×
10.2 cm)

Promised gift of Herb and
Lucy Pruzan

JAMES WASHINGTON JR.
BORN GLOSTER, MISSISSIPPI, 1909
DIED SEATTLE, WASHINGTON, 2000

*The Cup (Christ in
the Garden of
Gethsemane),* 1952
Encaustic paint on board
16 × 23½ inches (40.6 × 59.7 cm)

Gift of Paul I. Gingrich, Jr. in honor
of Barbara Johns, 2012.12

James Washington Jr. was a self-taught artist whose work reflects the folk traditions of his native Mississippi as well as his interest in religious and mystical themes. He began his artistic career as a painter, later becoming internationally known for his stone and wood sculptures of animals and portrait busts of prominent African Americans. Like his Northwest contemporary, Morris Graves (1910–2001), Washington was particularly fascinated with birds and they became frequent symbols in his works. In *The Cup,* Washington chose a religious subject, that of Christ seeing the vision of his coming crucifixion and death and struggling to accept his destiny.

JUAN ALONSO
BORN HAVANA, CUBA, 1956

El Guarachero, 1990
Acrylic on canvas with sequins
71 × 43 inches (180.3 × 109.2 cm)

Gift of Mary B. Browne and the
Francine Seders Gallery, 1996.1

Juan Alonso's work has taken many forms, from figurative to abstract, and though his techniques have varied he has stated that humanity is always the driving force. He has also often explored and celebrated his Latin American roots, with many works drawing on his Cuban heritage in terms of color, composition, or subject. *El Guarachero* depicts a member of Guaracheros de Regla, a dance troupe that formed in 1959 and became famous in the carnivals of Havana, Cuba. The expressive figure, bright costume, and addition of sequins to the canvas all evoke the colors and sounds of the festivals.

Artists' Biographies

VICTORIA ADAMS has earned critical acclaim and developed a passionate following of collectors and institutions nationwide for her luminous landscapes, which are steeped in the traditions of landscape painting and philosophy. In 1979 Adams completed a bachelor of fine arts degree from the University of Washington. Since her graduation, she has had more than 30 one-person exhibitions and been included in more than 65 group exhibitions in galleries in the United States and Canada. Tacoma Art Museum held a retrospective exhibition of her work in 2010. Her paintings are included in the collections of the Museum of Northwest Art in La Conner, the Boeing Company, the Allen Foundation for the Arts, the Nordstrom Corporation, the City of Chicago, and the US Department of State.

WAYNE ALBEE trained as a photographer beginning in his high school years in Tacoma, studying portraiture and working in a photographic supply store. In 1902 he opened his own photography studio; he later expanded the studio and renamed it Ye Likeness Shop, remaining in business in Tacoma until 1916. The following year Albee moved to Seattle and in 1919 joined the studio of photographer Ella McBride (1862–1965), who credited him with fostering her own interest in art photography. An influential pictorialist photographer, Albee also was a leading supporter of the short-lived but influential Seattle Camera Club in the mid- to late 1920s.

JUAN ALONSO came to the United States from Cuba as a child. After working as a professional musician, he began painting in the 1970s and decided to pursue a career as a professional artist. His work has been exhibited in galleries and museums throughout the United States, Canada, and Latin America. He was awarded a Neddy Artist Fellowship in 1997, the Morrie and Joan Alhadeff PONCHO Artist of the Year Award in 2007, and the Seattle Mayor's Arts Award in 2010. Alonso's work is in numerous public, private, and museum collections, and he has executed commissions in Seattle for the Qwest Stadium and Exhibition Center, the Port of Seattle, and Sound Transit, among others. He also has served as an advocate for Northwest artists and particularly for minority artists in Washington State.

GLEN ALPS received his bachelor of arts in education from Colorado State College (now Colorado State University) in 1940. After a brief stint teaching he decided to study art, receiving his master of fine arts from the University of Washington in 1947. Alps began teaching printmaking at the university while still working on his degree, and he continued in that role for almost 40 years, also serving as department head from 1979 to 1984. He was internationally known for his role in refining and popularizing the collagraph printmaking technique as well as championing the use of the silkscreen process in fine art. He exhibited work in Japan and Europe as well as across the United States, and his works can be found in numerous museum collections, including the Victoria and Albert Museum, London; the Museum of Modern Art, New York; and the Bibliothèque Nationale de France, Paris, among many others.

GUY ANDERSON showed an interest in art and other cultures from an early age. He studied with Eustace Ziegler (1881–1969) and in 1929 won a Tiffany & Co. Foundation scholarship to study painting at the Tiffany estate on Long Island, New York. On his return to Seattle, he worked a variety of jobs until 1939, when he was hired as an instructor at the Spokane Art Center, part of the

Works Progress Administration's Federal Art Project. After World War II, Anderson continued to support himself by teaching in Seattle and La Conner, Washington. He was awarded a Guggenheim Fellowship in 1975. Anderson is best known as one of the group of artists prominent in the mid-20th century labeled the Northwest Mystics—along with Kenneth Callahan (1905–1986), Morris Graves (1910–2001), and Mark Tobey (1890–1976)—because of their shared interests in Asian aesthetics, the spiritual or mystical possibilities of art, and muted colors.

ANNE APPLEBY received her master of fine arts from the San Francisco Art Institute in 1989. In addition to this formal training, she apprenticed for 15 years with a Native American artist, where she trained to be a detailed and committed observer. She has participated in group exhibitions at institutions that include Tacoma Art Museum, the American Academy in Rome, and the San Francisco Museum of Modern Art, where in 1996 she was awarded the SECA Art Award. She was also the 1999 recipient of the Biennial Award from the Louis Comfort Tiffany Foundation in New York and in 2006 received a Pollock-Krasner Foundation grant. Her works are in the collections of the San Francisco Museum of Modern Art, the Fine Arts Museums of San Francisco, the Albright-Knox Art Gallery in Buffalo, and the San Jose Museum of Art, among others.

ALFREDO ARREGUÍN attended the prestigious National Preparatory School in Mexico, where the renowned painter Diego Rivera (1886–1957) had been a teacher and the artist Frida Kahlo (1907–1954) a student. In 1956 Arreguín moved to Seattle to attend the University of Washington, where he received his bachelor of arts in 1967 and his master of fine arts in 1969; he later taught in the School of Art. In 1980 he received a fellowship from the National Endowment for the Arts and in 1995 received an Ohtli Award, which the Mexican government gives to distinguished individuals who contribute to Mexican culture abroad. In 2008 he was honored with a lifetime achievement award from the University of California, Riverside. His works are in the collections of the Smithsonian American Art Museum and the National Portrait Gallery.

RUDY AUTIO was a native of the Northwest, born in Montana, and he trained at Washington State University. Along with his friend and fellow ceramic innovator Peter Voulkos (1924–2002), he helped found the groundbreaking program at the Archie Bray Foundation for the Ceramic Arts in Helena, Montana, in 1951. He also served as head of the ceramics department at the University of Montana for 28 years.

JAY BACKSTRAND studied art at the Museum Art School at the Portland Art Museum (now the Pacific Northwest College of Art) from 1958 to 1961 and at Slade School of Fine Art, University College London, as a Fulbright fellow from 1964 to 1965. He went on to become an influential instructor in the Northwest, serving long tenures at both Portland State University and the Pacific Northwest College of Art. He also cofounded the Portland Center for the Visual Arts in 1971. In 1984 he was honored with a 10-year retrospective at Marylhurst University, Portland, Oregon, and was the subject of an exhibition at the Henry Art Gallery, University of Washington. His work is included in museum collections in the Northwest, Washington, DC, and England.

BO BARTLETT began his formal studies in Florence at the age of 19. On his return to the United States, he began taking classes at the University of the Arts in Philadelphia and then at the Pennsylvania Academy of the Fine Arts. He also studied anatomy at the Philadelphia College of Osteopathic Medicine. He later went on to study liberal arts at the University of Pennsylvania and filmmaking at New York University. His film *Snow Hill* about the artist Andrew Wyeth (1917–2009) started a lifelong relationship between the two artists, with Wyeth as mentor and friend. Bartlett has exhibited widely both nationally and internationally, and Bartlett and his paintings are featured in the Bo Bartlett Center as part of the Corn Center for Visual Arts, Columbus State University, Georgia.

RICK BARTOW earned a bachelor of arts in art education from Western Oregon University in 1969. After serving in the Vietnam War he returned to art making, building an impressive professional career. He has had solo exhibitions at museums, universities, and galleries internationally. His work was the subject of a retrospective organized by the Hallie Ford Museum of Art, Willamette University, in 2002, and he inaugurated the Continuum 12 series at the National Museum of the American Indian–Smithsonian Institution, New York, in 2003. In 2011 the A.D. Gallery, University of North Carolina, curated a major survey exhibition of his work. Honors include an Eiteljorg Museum Fellowship for Native American Fine Art and a year-long installation in the Jacqueline Kennedy Garden at the White House.

PAUL BERGER studied at the University of California, Los Angeles, and earned his master of fine arts from the Visual Studies Workshop at the State University of New York, Buffalo. He has been awarded two fellowships from the National Endowment for the Arts and helped establish the Photography Department at the University of Washington's School of Art in 1978, where he is currently the Donald E. Petersen Professor in the Arts. Berger has exhibited his work both nationally and in Europe and was the subject of a 2003 retrospective exhibition, *Persistence of Vision: The Art of Paul Berger, 1973–2003,* at the Museum of Contemporary Photography, Chicago. His work has been published in numerous texts on digital photography, and both his print and digital photography can be found in collections across the United States and in France.

LEO SAUL BERK earned a bachelor of fine arts in 1997 from the University of Illinois, Urbana-Champaign, and a master of fine arts in 1999 from the University of Washington. His work has been included in exhibitions locally at the Henry Art Gallery at the University of Washington, the Lee Center for the Arts at Seattle University, Cornish College of the Arts, Bellevue Arts Museum, and Frye Art Museum. Nationally, his work has been included in exhibitions at the California State University Art Museum in Long Beach and Dumbo Arts Center in Brooklyn. He has received major commissions from Sound Transit (University Link Light Rail Station), the King County Library System, Vulcan Inc., 4Culture, and the University of Washington as well as individual grants from 4Culture and Artist Trust. He was the recipient of the 2010 Arts Innovator Award from Artist Trust.

SONJA BLOMDAHL runs a glassblowing studio in Seattle and has served as an instructor at Pilchuck Glass School in Washington and Haystack Mountain School of Crafts in Maine. She received her bachelor of fine arts from the Massachusetts College of Art in 1974 and pursued further studies at the Orrefors Glass School in Sweden. She has an extensive exhibition record, including *Sonja Blomdahl: Incalmo* at the Montgomery Museum of Fine Arts in Alabama, a 20-year retrospective at the Museum of Northwest Art in La Conner, Washington, and notable group exhibitions such as *Masters of Contemporary Glass Art* at the Berkshire Museum in Pittsfield, Massachusetts, and *Taking Shape: The Pilchuck Glass School in the 70s* at Bellevue Art Museum (now Bellevue Arts Museum). Her work can be found in numerous museum and corporate collections.

FLORA BOOK started her career working at the McCall Pattern Company as a designer. In 1976 she began to develop her aesthetic vision while taking painting classes in Montreal, Quebec, at the Saidye Bronfman Centre for the Arts. During this time, she also studied fiber arts and jewelry. Her training continued at the University of Washington in 1980, where Book took classes from renowned jewelry artists Ramona Solberg (1921–2005) and Mary Lee Hu (born 1943). Book's jewelry has been collected by the Metropolitan Museum of Art and the Museum of Arts and Design in New York; the Museum of Fine Arts in Boston; the Detroit Institute of Arts; the Renwick Gallery, Smithsonian American Art Museum; Racine Art Museum in Wisconsin; and the Victoria and Albert Museum in London.

MICHAEL BROPHY graduated from the Pacific Northwest College of Art in Portland with a bachelor of fine arts in 1985. He has shown extensively in the Northwest, notably in one-person and group exhibitions in Seattle and Portland. He was the subject of a midcareer survey, *The Romantic Vision of Michael Brophy,* organized by Tacoma Art Museum in 2005, and was included in the recent surveys *Baja to Vancouver: The West Coast and Contemporary Art,* which opened at Seattle Art Museum in 2003, and *Critical Messages: Contemporary Northwest Artists on the Environment* at Boise Art Museum and the Western Gallery, Western Washington University, in Bellingham in 2010. He has received a

Pollock-Krasner Foundation grant and a National Endowment for the Arts Fellowship.

CRIS BRUCH earned both his master of arts and master of fine arts at the University of Wisconsin, Madison. He has presented one-person exhibitions at the Salt Lake Art Center, Suyama Space in Seattle, Port Angeles Fine Arts Center, Kirkland Fine Arts Center, and in Düsseldorf, Germany. His awards include the Betty Bowen Memorial Award, a Neddy Artist Fellowship in 2001, and a Pollock-Krasner Foundation grant in 2007. His work is included in the collections of the Henry Art Gallery at the University of Washington, New York Public Library Print Collection, Microsoft Art Collection, and Portland Art Museum. In 2006 Bruch installed a major outdoor sculpture for the Wayne Lyman Morse United States Courthouse in Eugene, Oregon, for which he garnered a 2008 General Services Administration Design Award for Excellence in Art and Architecture.

JOHN BUCK received his master of fine arts from the University of California, Davis. From 1976 to 1990 he taught sculpture at Montana State University, Bozeman. He has created commissioned works for institutions across the West, including Lewis and Clark College in Portland, Children's Hospital in Denver, and Swedish Hospital in Seattle, and nationally in Minnesota and Ohio. He has had solo exhibitions in New York, Colorado, California, Florida, and Oregon, including *John Buck: Iconography* that traveled to Washington, Indiana, Iowa, and Montana in 2009 and 2010. His work can be found in museum collections across the United States, including the Brooklyn Museum, Denver Art Museum, and the Museum of Contemporary Art, Chicago, among many others.

LOUIS BUNCE began his art training at the Museum Art School at the Portland Art Museum (now the Pacific Northwest College of Art); then, in 1927, he went to New York to attend the Art Students League. It was during this time that he established his lifelong connections to the New York art scene, including friends such as Jackson Pollock (1912–1956) and the sculptor David Smith (1906–1965). Starting in 1939, Bunce worked for the Works Progress Administration's Federal Art Project as a painter and as a teacher at the Salem Art Center, Oregon. He moved to Portland in the early 1940s and after World War II became a faculty member at the Museum Art School, where he taught for almost 30 years, influencing generations of students.

MARSHA BURNS has earned a number of honors over the course of her long career. Her photographs can be found in distinguished museum collections, including the Museum of Modern Art and the Metropolitan Museum of Art in New York, the Center for Creative Photography at the University of Arizona, and the Stedelijk Museum in Amsterdam, among others. She has received two fellowships from the National Endowment for the Arts and has exhibited her work in both solo and group exhibitions regionally and nationally. Burns received her training from the University of Washington and the University of Massachusetts.

MARK CALDERON received his bachelor of arts from San Jose State University, California, in 1978. He has had solo exhibitions in Seattle and Portland, Oregon, as well as in New York and Philadelphia. He has created a number of public works for the Seattle Arts Commission, Artist Trust, Sound Transit, and the City of Seattle. Calderon received a Betty Bowen Memorial Award in 1986, a WESTAF/NEA Regional Fellowship for Visual Arts for Distinguished Achievement in Sculpture in 1993, and a Painters and Sculptors Grant Program Award from the Joan Mitchell Foundation, New York, in 2001. His work can be found in numerous public and corporate collections in the Northwest and in Boise Art Museum, the Burke Museum of Natural History and Culture at the University of Washington, and the Philadelphia Museum of Art.

KENNETH CALLAHAN served as a catalyst for Seattle artists in the mid-20th century through his own painting, his work as assistant director of Seattle Art Museum, and his writings about contemporary art. Born in Spokane and largely self-taught as an artist, Callahan was committed to an art that went beyond the merely illustrative. He enrolled at the University of Washington in 1924 but did not complete a degree. After leaving the university he traveled widely, absorbing influences from the different countries and cultures he experienced. His talent was recognized early; his work was included in the first Whitney Biennial exhibition in 1933 and he went on to a distinguished painting career. Callahan is identified as one of the Northwest Mystics—along with Guy Anderson (1906–1998), Morris Graves (1910–2001), and Mark Tobey (1890–1976)—who shared a muted palette and strong interest in Asian aesthetics.

MARGARET CAMFFERMAN studied at the Minneapolis School of Fine Arts, the New York School of Applied Arts and Design, and with modernist painter Robert Henri (1865–1929). When she and her husband, Peter Camfferman (1890–1957), settled in the Seattle area in 1915, they became members of Seattle's avant-garde art association called the Group of Twelve. Camfferman also was an early member of the Women Painters of Washington. She had an active Northwest exhibition history, including a solo exhibition at Seattle Art Museum in 1935 and an exhibition at the Legion of Honor, San Francisco. She also was a dedicated teacher. She and her husband established an art colony at their home on Whidbey Island and had close ties to the art department at the University of Washington.

PETER CAMFFERMAN was a landscape painter, etcher, and art educator. He trained at the Minneapolis School of Fine Art and with the French cubist painter and sculptor André Lhote (1885–1962) at the Lhote Atelier in Paris. Camfferman and his artist wife, Margaret Camfferman (1881–1964), arrived in the Northwest in 1915, settling at Langley, Whidbey Island, where they established an art colony at their home, Brachenwood. The colony flourished from the 1920s through Peter Camfferman's death in 1957.

JAMES CASTLE was a self-taught artist who worked with materials he found around his home, mostly waste paper and stove soot mixed with saliva, repeatedly drawing his surroundings and other rural scenes. Deaf since birth, Castle did not learn to sign, fingerspell, or read and write but seems to have primarily used his drawings to communicate. His work was not exhibited during his lifetime. In recent years Castle's work has been collected by the Art Institute of Chicago and, in New York, by the Museum of American Folk Art, the Museum of Modern Art, and the Whitney Museum of American Art, in addition to numerous regional institutions. A major retrospective exhibition was organized by the Philadelphia Museum of Art in 2009 and traveled around the country.

FRANCIS CELENTANO earned his bachelor's degree in 1951 and master's degree in 1957, both from the Institute of Fine Arts at New York University. He was awarded a Fulbright Fellowship and spent a year in Rome, painting and traveling in Italy, France, and Spain. He originally painted in an abstract expressionist style but gradually embraced the op art movement during the 1960s. In 1966 Celentano assumed a full-time teaching position in the School of Art at the University of Washington, where he taught for 30 years and is now professor emeritus. A major retrospective exhibition of his work was organized by the Hallie Ford Museum of Art, Willamette University, in 2010.

DALE CHIHULY, born in 1941 in Tacoma, started his career in architecture and interior design before studying glass with renowned artist and educator Harvey Littleton (born 1922) at the University of Wisconsin, Madison, in the mid-1960s. Chihuly's innovations moved glass sculpture off the pedestal and into large-scale sculptural installations. He also explored sculptural interventions on walls or ceilings, suspended from bridges, and perched in natural outdoor settings. Highlights of his distinguished career include *Chihuly in the Light of Jerusalem 2000*; *Mille Fiori Venezia* at the 53rd Venice Biennale in 2009, an installation first presented at Tacoma Art Museum in 2003; a retrospective exhibition at the Museum of Fine Arts, Boston, in 2011; and *100,000 Pounds of Ice and Neon* at the Tacoma Dome in 1993. In May 2012, Chihuly Garden and Glass opened in Seattle, a permanent installation of a diverse body of his work.

FAY CHONG emigrated to Seattle from his native China in 1920. He studied art at Seattle's Broadway High School alongside sculptor George Tsutakawa (1910–1997) and painter Morris Graves (1910–2001). He also studied informally with the artist Mark Tobey (1890–1976) and later received a bachelor of arts and master of arts in art education from the University of Washington. Chong exhibited his work throughout the Northwest as well as at the

Santa Barbara Museum of Art and in Philadelphia and New York. He was active in a number of Washington art associations, including the Puget Sound Group of Painters and the Northwest Printmakers Society and, along with Tsutakawa, formed the Chinese Arts Club.

CHUCK CLOSE was a student at the University of Washington from 1958 to 1962, where he developed a style of abstraction deeply influenced by prominent artists such as Hans Hofmann (1880–1966) and Willem de Kooning (1904–1997). After earning his master of fine arts from Yale University, Close began painting large-scale photorealist portraits of his artist colleagues, friends, and family based on photographs he enlarged using a grid system. These portraits quickly established Close as one of the nation's most prestigious artists. In the late 1990s he began working with daguerreotypes (an early photographic process), using these images to create a series of digital pigment prints, tapestries, and photogravures.

BILL COLBY received his bachelor of arts from the University of Denver in 1950 and his master of arts from the University of Illinois in 1954. From 1956 through 1989, he was first a professor of art and then professor emeritus at the University of Puget Sound in Tacoma. In the mid-1960s he was director of Tacoma Art Museum, and from 1988 to 1991 he served as a lecturer for the Washington State Commission for the Humanities on Chinese and Japanese printmaking. Colby has an extensive exhibition history, including regional and national group print exhibitions as well as solo exhibitions throughout the Northwest.

ROBERT COLESCOTT received his bachelor's degree from the University of California, Berkeley, in 1949 and then traveled to Paris to spend a year studying with the cubist painter and sculptor Fernand Léger (1881–1955). Colescott returned to the United States to pursue his master of fine arts degree at Berkeley. After graduating in 1952 he began teaching art for Seattle Public Schools and then at Portland State University. In the late 1960s he began to earn critical acclaim for his depictions of the African American experience, often cast as funny and ironic retellings of history. These brightly colored images, bordering on caricatures, became his mature signature style. Among his many extraordinary accomplishments, Colescott was the first African American artist to represent the United States in a solo exhibition at the Venice Biennale in 1997.

KEN CORY received his bachelor of fine arts in 1966 from the California College of Arts and Crafts and his master of fine arts in 1969 from Washington State University. He taught at Central Washington State College (now Central Washington University) in Ellensburg for several decades, training generations of Northwest jewelers and sculptors. His interest in using found objects and incorporating humor into his works helped spark a new style in Northwest jewelry making. A major retrospective exhibition of his work titled *The Jewelry of Ken Cory: Play Disguised* was held at Tacoma Art Museum in 1997.

CLAIRE COWIE studied printmaking at Washington University, St. Louis, and earned a master of fine arts degree from the University of Washington in 1999. She had a one-person exhibition, *Claire Cowie: Flying Ladies of Leisure,* and was artist in residence at the Henry Art Gallery, University of Washington, in 2003. She received a Neddy Artist Fellowship in 2004 and a Pollock-Krasner Foundation grant in 2005. Her work is in corporate and museum collections in Seattle, Tacoma, and St. Louis.

WILLIAM CUMMING was primarily self-taught. He briefly attended the Northwest Academy of Art in Seattle and took some correspondence courses, but he learned mainly through observation, practice, and critiques from fellow artists. He worked as a commercial illustrator and then as an art and music reviewer for Seattle's *Town Crier* before being hired for the Works Progress Administration's Federal Art Project, where he met the artist Morris Graves (1910–2001) who in turn introduced him to a number of other Seattle artists. Cumming had his first solo exhibition at Seattle Art Museum in 1941 but soon thereafter his career was interrupted by a serious illness. In the 1950s he began actively teaching, painting, and exhibiting again, including a second solo exhibition at Seattle Art Museum in 1961. He went on to exhibit in numerous solo and group exhibitions, and his work can be found in public, private, and museum collections throughout the region.

IMOGEN CUNNINGHAM, pioneering Northwest photographer, trained in the Seattle studio of Edward S. Curtis (1868–1952)—best known for his 20-volume photographic series *The North American Indian*—before establishing her own photography business. Her studio became a gathering place for Seattle's progressive artists, many of whom served as models. Cunningham relocated to California in 1917. From 1932 to 1934 she photographed politicians and Hollywood movie stars for the magazine *Vanity Fair.* She continued to create her own artistic work as well and was a founding member of the important San Francisco–based photography collective Group f/64. Her work was critical in defining the look of modern photography in the first half of the 20th century.

MARGARET DE PATTA was a pioneer in the American studio art jewelry movement on the West Coast. She trained at the California School of Fine Arts (now the San Francisco Art Institute) and the Art Students League, New York. She moved to the San Francisco Bay area in 1923 and began making rings, bracelets, and necklaces that reflected modernist ideas. A mentor and teacher to many Bay Area jewelers, she also was a founding member of the San Francisco Metal Arts Guild. Her work can be found in the collections of the Oakland Museum; the British Museum in London; the Museum of Fine Arts in Boston; the Renwick Gallery, Smithsonian American Art Museum; and the Museum of Arts and Design in New York.

DENNIS EVANS is one of a group of University of Washington art students from the mid-1970s who reinvigorated the regional artist community. Starting as a chemistry student, Evans then discovered ceramics and in 1973 earned a bachelor of fine arts at the University of Washington, where he also earned his master of fine arts in 1975. In the late 1970s Evans combined his interests in ceramics, philosophy, mythology, and art into ritual performances. These events quickly captured local and national attention and led to his inclusion in the 1978 Whitney Biennial. In addition to his performances, he has made a career creating installations and mixed-media works that incorporate both painting and sculpture and include layers of objects, text, and symbols. His works are included in collections across the Northwest as well as in the Museum of Modern Art and the Metropolitan Museum of Art in New York.

JOE FEDDERSEN studied art at Wenatchee Valley College and the University of Washington, receiving his master of fine arts from the University of Wisconsin, Madison, in 1989. After graduation he served as a member of the art faculty at The Evergreen State College in Olympia from 1989 to 2009. Feddersen has had 29 one-person exhibitions, including *Continuum 12 Artists: Joe Feddersen* at the National Museum of the American Indian–Smithsonian Institution in New York; and the exhibition *Vital Signs* organized by the Hallie Ford Museum of Art, Willamette University, and on view at Tacoma Art Museum in 2009. Since 1982 his work has been included in more than 125 group exhibitions across the United States and in Germany. Locally, he was juried into the Northwest Biennial in 1995 and 2007 and was artist in residence at the Museum of Glass, Tacoma, in 2005 and 2009. His work can be found in museums throughout the United States.

SCOTT FIFE, a realist sculptor and Seattle artist, earned a bachelor of arts in architecture from the University of Idaho in 1972 and a bachelor of arts from the Minneapolis College of Art and Design in 1976. He was granted fellowships by the New York Foundation for the Arts in 1989 and Artist Trust in 1999. Galleries and museums have hosted his one-person exhibitions since the mid-1970s, and he regularly exhibited in Berlin in the 1980s and 1990s. Tacoma Art Museum held a retrospective exhibition of his work in 2004 and Missoula Art Museum, Montana, hosted a solo show of his work in 2010.

CLAUDIA FITCH studied painting at the University of Washington and earned her master of fine arts in 1979 from the Tyler School of Art at Temple University in Philadelphia. Her one-person exhibitions include shows at the European Ceramic Work Centre in Hertogenbosch, the Netherlands; the Munson-Williams-Proctor Arts Institute, Utica, New York; and in New York City at P.S. 122, the New Museum, and Franklin Furnace. She has shown frequently at museums in Washington State, including Bellevue Art Museum (now Bellevue Arts Museum) and Seattle Art Museum. In 2003 she completed commissions for Metro King County and Qwest

Field. Fitch was the recipient of a Pollock-Krasner Foundation grant in 1997 and a Neddy Artist Fellowship in 2000.

JAMES FITZGERALD studied art at the University of Washington, the Kansas City Art Institute, and briefly with Thomas Hart Benton (1889–1975) at the Art Center School in Los Angeles. In the 1940s he traveled to Mexico to study mural painting under José Clemente Orozco (1883–1949). FitzGerald taught at his alma maters in Kansas and Washington State and served as director of the Spokane Art Center under the government's Federal Art Project in 1941. During this period he also created work for Works Progress Administration art projects in Colorado, Washington, and California. He exhibited extensively across the United States, including group exhibitions at the Whitney Museum of American Art in New York, the Art Institute of Chicago, and the Albright-Knox Art Gallery in Buffalo and solo exhibitions at Seattle Art Museum, the Santa Barbara Museum of Art, and San Francisco Art Museum (now the San Francisco Museum of Modern Art).

WILLIAM GIVLER was one of Oregon's most influential artists and teachers. He worked at the Museum Art School at the Portland Art Museum for 42 years, first as an instructor and then as dean from 1944 until 1973. Under his leadership, the school (now the Pacific Northwest College of Art) was accredited and established a four-year degree program. In addition to his distinguished career as an educator and mentor, Givler was also a dedicated painter and printmaker who inaugurated Oregon's Print Annual exhibitions. Prolific despite his busy teaching career, he exhibited his works widely in regional exhibitions. Givler also worked briefly for the federal government's Public Works of Art Project in Oregon in 1934, making art for government and other public buildings.

KATHRYN GLOWEN trained in fine art and graphic design at Washington State University and the University of Tulsa. She has had solo exhibitions throughout the Northwest, notably her major installation *Petland: One Woman's Century* in 1997 that traveled to 13 different venues across Washington State and to Fort Wayne, Indiana. She also has participated in numerous group exhibitions in the Northwest, Midwest, and Asia. Glowen works primarily with assemblages of found objects and with textiles, and she has created a variety of public commissions around Washington, including for the King County Justice Center and Swedish Medical Center, both in Seattle; and the Sound Transit station in Auburn.

JOSEPH GOLDBERG was one of the first Northwest painters to embrace a reductive aesthetic. His work can be found in numerous corporate and public collections in Seattle and the greater Puget Sound region. The Museum of Northwest Art in La Conner, Washington held a retrospective exhibition of his work in 2007, and he had a solo exhibition in 1987 at the Sheehan Gallery, Whitman College, in Walla Walla. Group exhibitions include the

Jundt Art Museum at Gonzaga University in Spokane, Bellevue Art Museum (now Bellevue Arts Museum), Tacoma Art Museum, and the American Academy and Institute of Arts and Letters in New York. Goldberg received the Betty Bowen Memorial Award in 1980.

LAYNE GOLDSMITH received her master of fine arts from Cranbrook Academy of Art, Bloomfield, Michigan, in 1979. She has been a faculty member in the University of Washington's fibers program since 1983 and also has served as chair. In addition to her academic work she is an active studio artist with work in numerous public collections, such as those of the Washington State Arts Commission and King County Arts Commission; in the corporate collections of the Hartford Insurance Group and AT&T; and in the Cranbrook Academy of Art Museum, among others. She also has actively exhibited her work both nationally, at such institutions as the American Craft Museum (now the Museum of Arts and Design) in New York, Bellevue Arts Museum, the Detroit Institute of Arts, the Rochester Institute of Technology, and the Wadsworth Atheneum Museum of Art in Hartford, Connecticut, as well as internationally at venues in Colombia, France, Scotland, and Israel. In 2005 Goldsmith formed Dorjé Contemporary, a carpet design and production company.

JOHN GRADE studied at the Pratt Institute, Brooklyn, New York, graduating with his bachelor of fine arts in 1992. He has had solo exhibitions and sited installations of his work both regionally and in Atlanta, Georgia, and Valenciennes, France. In 2011 he was included in the Contemporary Northwest Art Awards exhibition at Portland Art Museum, Oregon, and has participated in group shows in Wisconsin and California and throughout the Northwest. He has received numerous grants from Artist Trust and 4Culture and has been awarded grants from the Pollock-Krasner Foundation and Louis Comfort Tiffany Foundation. In 2010 he received the Willard L. Metcalf Award in Art from the American Academy of Arts and Letters, New York.

MORRIS GRAVES was one of the more enigmatic figures in Northwest art history. A self-taught artist, he dropped out of high school to sail on American Mail Line ships across the Pacific Ocean, giving him a taste for travel that lasted throughout his lifetime and introducing him to the culture and art of Japan, where he discovered a strong aesthetic affiliation. Though he was reluctant to exhibit his work, friends managed to convince him, and his inclusion in an exhibition at the Museum of Modern Art in 1942 brought him to national attention. Graves was one of the group of artists dubbed the Northwest Mystics—along with Guy Anderson (1906–1998), Kenneth Callahan (1905–1986), and Mark Tobey (1890–1976)—so-called for the philosophical and spiritual content of their works.

HADLEY + MAXWELL has collaborated and exhibited work in Canada, the United States, and abroad since 1998. Born in 1973

and 1966 respectively, the duo has created film sets, opera and dance productions, and conceptual works in all media. In 2005 they were recipients of the prestigious VIVA Award. Their work was the subject of a solo exhibition, *Deleted Scenes,* at the Contemporary Art Gallery in Vancouver, British Columbia, in 2006. That same year, work from their *Décor* series was included in Habitat at Jessica Bradley Art + Projects in Toronto. In December 2007 their video work was included in the Art Basel Miami video lounge.

VIRNA HAFFER, from Tacoma, was one of the most diverse artists in the Northwest in the first half of the 20th century. In a career spanning more than six decades, she found success as a printmaker, painter, musician, sculptor, and author. However, she devoted most of her creative energy to photography, the medium that best satisfied her many interests. Essentially self-taught as a photographer, she learned through observation, trial and error, and assistantships with local photographers. Although she lived far from the major art centers of the East Coast and Europe, Haffer became an internationally recognized photographer, known particularly for her innovative work in the 1960s with photograms, a form of camera-less photography. She also ran a successful commercial portrait studio that supported her creative work.

CARL HALL trained at the Meinzinger School in Detroit before interrupting a promising artistic career to enlist in the army during World War II. As an infantryman he visited Oregon and fell in love with the landscape, returning there permanently after the war in 1946. He began teaching at Willamette University in Salem, at first part-time and then as a full professor, a position he held for 40 years. His works can be found in numerous regional collections and in the collections of the Museum of Fine Arts, Boston; the Corcoran Gallery of Art, Washington, DC; the Whitney Museum of American Art, New York; and the Detroit Institute of Arts. Despite his national reputation, Hall chose to remain in Salem throughout his career.

THOMAS HANDFORTH, from Tacoma, was a painter and watercolorist but is perhaps best known for his prints and work as an author and illustrator of children's books. Handforth was classically trained at the National Academy of Design and the Art Students League in New York as well as at the École des Beaux-Arts in Paris. He also studied with Tacoma painter Alice Engley Beek (1867–1951). Handforth was a world traveler, visiting Morocco, Mexico, China, and Canada and creating images of their citizens and lifeways. He received a Guggenheim Fellowship for his creative work in China and a Caldecott Award for his book *Mei Li* in 1939.

GAYLEN HANSEN earned his master of fine arts in 1953 from the University of Southern California and went on to teach in the art department at Washington State University for 25 years, retiring in 1982. In addition to his teaching, he has been highly prolific and an active participant in the contemporary art scene, exhibiting in Berlin, Singapore, and Beijing as well as in cities across the United States, including New York, Los Angeles, and Seattle. Hansen was the recipient of a 1989 Governor's Arts Award from the State of Washington and a 2001 Flintridge Foundation Award for Visual Artists. His work can be found in public and private collections nationwide. Seattle Art Museum held a retrospective exhibition of his work in 2008.

RANDY HAYES earned a bachelor of fine arts degree in 1968 from Memphis Academy of Art (now the Memphis College of Art). After working as a scene painter and designer for public television in Boston, he returned to Seattle and opened a bookstore and gallery. In 1979 he began a series of paintings and pastel drawings of boxers and other everyday people who lived slightly outside the mainstream. In 1990, after working in a variety of media, he began to paint directly onto grids of photographs, exploring the relationship between painting and photography. Hayes has had many solo exhibitions at museums, including Boise Art Museum, Seattle Art Museum, the Cheekwood Museum in Nashville, and Bellevue Arts Museum, and his work can be found in numerous public and corporate collections. In 1982 he received the Betty Bowen Memorial Award and in 2003 and 2004 a Flintridge Foundation Award for Visual Artists.

Z. VANESSA HELDER studied at the University of Washington and at the Art Students League in New York. In 1939 she taught at the Spokane Art Center under the sponsorship of the Federal Art Project of the Works Progress Administration and also created a series of watercolors documenting construction of the Grand Coulee Dam. In 1943 she relocated to Los Angeles, where she remained for the rest of her life. Helder's work was widely exhibited at such prestigious venues as New York's Museum of Modern Art, Whitney Museum of American Art, and Metropolitan Museum of Art as well as at Oakland Art Museum and Denver Art Museum. She had a one-person exhibition at Seattle Art Museum in 1939 and was included in the important *Realists and Magic Realists* exhibition at the Museum of Modern Art, New York, in 1943. Helder also was a member of the Women Painters of Washington, the National Association of Women Artists, and the American and California Watercolor Societies.

ROBERT HELM earned his master of fine arts in 1969 from Washington State University, studying in part with the Northwest painter Gaylen Hansen (born 1921). He taught briefly at the University of Colorado and then at Washington State University from 1971 to 1984. Helm was a meticulous painter, creating only a few works each year that were exhibited in New York, Los Angeles, Seattle, and Berlin. A retrospective of his work was held at Tacoma Art Museum in 1995. He received a Governor's Arts Award from the State of Washington in 1992 and a Flintridge Foundation Award for Visual Artists in 2004.

MARY HENRY received her bachelor of fine arts from the California School of Arts and Crafts (now California College of the Arts) in 1934. After attending a lecture by Bauhaus artist László Moholy-Nagy (1894–1946), she went to study with him at the Institute of Design, Chicago, receiving her master of arts in the late 1940s. Her career as a professional artist stretched over eight decades and she exhibited widely. Henry's work was the subject of a major retrospective in 2007 at the Wright Exhibition Space, Seattle, and in 2009 at the Sun Valley Center for the Arts, Idaho. In 2001 she received a Flintridge Foundation Award for Visual Artists, and in 2006 she received the Twining Humber Award for Lifetime Artistic Achievement from Artist Trust. Her work can be found in museums throughout the Northwest and at the IIT Institute of Design, Chicago.

JIM HODGES is an internationally known artist with roots in Washington State. He received his bachelor of fine arts from Fort Wright College in Spokane in 1980 and his master of fine arts from the Pratt Institute in Brooklyn in 1986. He has had numerous solo exhibitions both nationally and internationally, including at the Centre Pompidou in Paris, and has created a number of large-scale installations for public sites, including at the Hirshhorn Museum and Sculpture Garden in Washington, DC, and the Albright-Knox Art Gallery in Buffalo. He has received grants and awards from the Washington State Arts Commission, the Penny McCall Foundation, the Louis Comfort Tiffany Foundation, and the Association Internationale des Critiques d'Art.

SARAH HOOD earned a bachelor of arts with an emphasis on writing from Eugene Lang College at the New School in New York, while studying metalsmithing at Parsons the New School for Design as part of their product design program. She went on to earn a postbaccalaureate bachelor of fine arts from the University of Washington. Her work has been shown at the Savannah College of Art and Design, the Fuller Craft Museum in Brockton, Massachusetts, Velvet da Vinci in San Francisco, and The Gallery at the Museum of Contemporary Craft in Portland, Oregon, and has been included in numerous jewelry publications.

WILLIAM HOPPE is an associate professor of art at Central Oregon Community College in Bend, where he has been teaching since 2000. He received his bachelor of arts in 1967 from St. John's University, New York, and his master of fine arts in 1973 from the University of Washington. After working in New York City for 10 years, he relocated to the Northwest. Hoppe has exhibited widely and his abstract paintings can be found in numerous museum, corporate, and private collections in the Northwest. He also has created large-scale murals for public buildings in the region, including the Nordstrom Medical Tower in Seattle and the Oregon Convention Center in Portland.

PAUL HORIUCHI studied sumi painting as a teenager in his native Japan. When he immigrated to the United States in 1922, he began working for the Union Pacific Railroad but continued to paint in his free time. He and his growing family survived World War II supported by his odd jobs and help from friends. His painting career began to take off in the mid-1940s and particularly after 1950, when an accident forced him to more actively market his paintings for sale, bringing them to the attention of a broader audience of collectors, gallerists, and curators.

MARY LEE HU was introduced to metalsmithing in high school. She went on to receive a bachelor of fine arts in 1965 from Cranbrook Academy of Art in Bloomfield, Michigan, and a master of fine arts in 1967 from Southern Illinois University focused on jewelry and small-scale metal objects. She has taught extensively, including at the University of Iowa, Kansas State University, and University of Wisconsin, and she has been a professor at the University of Washington since 1980. Hu has exhibited her work widely both nationally and internationally and it has been extensively published. She is also an active member and past president of the Society of North American Goldsmiths.

YVONNE TWINING HUMBER, a New York City native, pursued her art training at the National Academy of Design and at the Art Students League. From 1935 to 1943 she worked for the Federal Art Project in Boston, establishing a national reputation. After relocating to Seattle in 1943 she continued to exhibit nationally at such prestigious venues as the Phillips Memorial Gallery in Washington, DC, and the Palace of the Legion of Honor in San Francisco. She was also active regionally, joining and later becoming president of the Women Painters of Washington as well as the Northwest Printmakers Society. Seattle Art Museum had a solo exhibition of her work in 1946. Artist Trust in Seattle annually awards a prize she endowed to recognize Washington State women artists over the age of 60.

WALTER ISAACS trained at the Academie Colarossi in Paris during the 1920s and then came to the University of Washington upon the invitation of Henry Suzzallo, then president of the university. Isaacs served as teacher in and ultimately director of the University of Washington School of Art from 1923 to 1954. His leadership was instrumental in the development of the art department and he was a major influence on three generations of students. His paintings and teachings were grounded in the formal principles of the French postimpressionist painters, such as Paul Cézanne (1839–1906) and Henri Matisse (1869–1954), whom he had studied in Paris. He also served as director of the Henry Art Gallery at the university for many years.

WILLIAM IVEY began studying art in 1941 at Cornish College of the Arts in Seattle but was soon drafted into the US Army. After his discharge in 1946 he enrolled at the California School of Fine Arts (now the San Francisco Art Institute). He returned to Seattle in 1948. Ivey had one-person exhibitions at Seattle Art Museum in 1964 and 1975 and at the Henry Art Gallery, University

of Washington, in 1989. He received a Ford Foundation Purchase Award in 1960, a National Foundation for the Arts and Humanities grant in 1962, and a Rockefeller Fellowship in 1967. He is considered one of the Northwest's most accomplished abstract expressionist painters.

MANUEL IZQUIERDO began his art training at the École Supérieur des Beaux-Arts in Marseilles before relocating to the United States. He took classes at the Museum Art School at the Portland Art Museum (now the Pacific Northwest College of Art) as well as with sculptor Hilda Morris (1911–1991) and with Lloyd Reynolds (1902–1978), a nationally known calligrapher and printmaker who taught Izquierdo how to make wood engravings. Izquierdo was instrumental in raising the profile of abstract sculpture in the Northwest through exhibitions of his work, numerous public art commissions, and his 46-year career as a teacher at the Museum Art School. He also was a prolific printmaker, focusing on figurative subjects, a counterpoint to the increasingly abstract look of his sculptures.

BILL JACOBSON lived and worked in Seattle in 1978 before attending the San Francisco Art Institute, where he earned his master of fine arts in 1981. He has had numerous solo exhibitions of his work and has participated in group exhibitions throughout the United States and Europe. He has been artist in residence at MacDowell Colony, New Hampshire; Blue Mountain Center, New York; and the Edward Albee Foundation, New York. Multiple monographs have been published on his work.

DOUG JECK attended the School of the Art Institute of Chicago and earned a master of fine arts in 1989. He has had one-person exhibitions at galleries in Seattle, San Francisco, Chicago, and Atlanta. His work is in the collections of the Schein-Joseph International Museum of Ceramic Art in Alfred, New York; the Los Angeles County Museum of Art; the Renwick Gallery, Smithsonian American Art Museum; the Mint Museum of Craft and Design in Charlotte, North Carolina; and Seattle Art Museum. His work has been reviewed in numerous journals, including *Art in America, New Art Examiner, Sculpture, American Ceramics,* and *Ceramics Monthly.* He has received several fellowships from the National Endowment for the Arts and awards from La Napoule Art Foundation and the Virginia A. Groot Foundation. He has taught ceramics at the University of Washington since 1996.

DOROTHY DOLPH JENSEN was sent to study art in Antwerp, Belgium, at the age of 12 and then continued at the prestigious Académie Julian in Paris. Upon returning to the Northwest, she studied at the Museum Art School at the Portland Art Museum (now the Pacific Northwest College of Art) with the influential artist and teacher Henry F. "Harry" Wentz (1875–1965). After relocating to Seattle, Jensen went on to a nationally successful career as a painter. She was a founding member of the Women Painters of Washington and a charter member of the Northwest Watercolor

Society. Jensen was also one of the Northwest's earliest and most dedicated printmakers. She exhibited her work nationally, including in Seattle, Los Angeles, Chicago, and Washington, DC.

FAY JONES earned her bachelor of fine arts from the Rhode Island School of Design in 1957. During her extensive and prolific career she has received two fellowships from the National Endowment for the Arts; has been artist in residence at Pilchuck Glass School in Stanwood, Washington, the University of Nebraska, Omaha, and the La Napoule Art Foundation in France; and has participated in both solo and group exhibitions across the Northwest. Boise Art Museum organized a major retrospective exhibition in 1996. Her works can be found in numerous public and private collections in the Northwest and include public commissions such as the monumental mural for the Westlake Transit Station in downtown Seattle. In 2005 she received the Twining Humber Award for Lifetime Artistic Achievement from Artist Trust in Seattle.

ROBERT C. JONES, a longtime instructor at the University of Washington, is one of the Northwest's most respected and influential teachers. He earned a bachelor of fine arts and a master of science from the Rhode Island School of Design. He has had one-person exhibitions at the Whatcom Museum of History and Art (now the Whatcom Museum) in Bellingham, Seattle Art Museum, Tacoma Art Museum, and the Museum of Northwest Art in La Conner. Jones has received a National Endowment for the Arts Fellowship and a Flintridge Foundation Award for Visual Artists. His works can be found in the collections of the City of Seattle, Safeco Corporation, Microsoft Corporation, and the Hallie Ford Museum of Art at Willamette University.

MEL KATZ trained at Cooper Union, New York, and the Brooklyn Museum Art School in the mid-1950s before moving to Oregon in 1964 to teach at the Museum Art School at the Portland Art Museum (now the Pacific Northwest College of Art). A year later he transferred to Portland State University, where he taught for more than 30 years. In addition to participating in numerous group exhibitions, Katz also has had solo exhibitions in Portland, Seattle, and San Francisco, including a retrospective at Portland Art Museum in 1988. He won the Oregon Governor's Arts Award in 1999. His work can be found in public and private collections throughout the Northwest, and he has executed commissions for a number of public buildings.

ARNOLD J. KEMP is a painter, photographer, and poet who received his joint bachelor of arts/bachelor of fine arts in 1991 from Tufts University, Massachusetts, and the School of the Museum of Fine Arts, Boston, and his master of fine arts from Stanford University in 2005. He has had solo exhibitions at the San Francisco African American Historical Society, Gallery ESP, and the Quotidian Gallery in San Francisco and the Portland Institute of Contemporary Art in Oregon; and he has participated in group exhibitions both nationally and internationally. He has received a number of awards, including a Painters and Sculptors Grant Program Award from the Joan Mitchell Foundation, a residency at Cité Internationale des Arts in Paris, and in 2012 he was named a Guggenheim Fellow for the Fine Arts. He currently manages the master of fine arts program for the Pacific Northwest College of Art in Portland, Oregon.

MICHAEL KENNA has had more than 500 one-person and group exhibitions at galleries and museums worldwide. He studied at the London College of Printing, the Banbury School of Art in Oxfordshire, and St. Joseph's College in Lancashire. His work is included in the collections of the Bibliothèque Nationale de France in Paris, the Tokyo Metropolitan Museum of Photography, the National Gallery of Art in Washington, DC, Shanghai Art Museum, and the Victoria and Albert Museum in London, among others. Numerous books on his work have been published over the past 25 years.

MAUDE KERNS was born into an early pioneer family in Oregon. As good schools were scarce on the frontier, she moved to New York in the early 1900s to study at the Columbia University Teachers College. There she met and studied art with the modernist Arthur Wesley Dow (1857–1922). After graduation she moved first to Seattle and then to Eugene to teach art at the University of Oregon, where she worked until 1947. She later founded the Eugene Art Center, renamed the Maude Kerns Art Center in 1961. Throughout her career, she continued to travel and study both in Europe and the United States, keeping abreast of the latest trends in contemporary art.

JOHN FRANKLIN KOENIG came to know and love French culture while serving in the army during World War II. After the war he studied French language and literature as well as design and art at the University of Washington. During this period he also became involved in the Seattle art scene, coming to know artists such as Mark Tobey (1890–1976) and Morris Graves (1910–2001). In 1948 he moved to Paris, where he lived and worked for 30 years, also opening a gallery. He later began spending part of each year in Seattle. In 1986 he was made a Commander of the French Order of Arts and Letters. Koenig's work has been exhibited and collected internationally, particularly in France and Japan. Several museums have held retrospectives of his work, including the Paris Art Center, Seattle Art Museum, and the Museum of Northwest Art in La Conner.

DR. KYO KOIKE was a physician who immigrated to the United States in 1916, settling in Seattle. He actively pursued his many artistic interests, including poetry, prose writing, and photography. He taught himself to write in English and then translated more than 30 volumes of literature from Japanese. Koike began exhibiting his photography in 1920 at the Frederick and Nelson Salons in Seattle and then in national and international competitions, quickly rising to prominence in pictorialist circles. In 1924 he cofounded the Seattle Camera Club and became the editor of the club's bilingual monthly bulletin, *Notan*, published from 1925 to 1929. His works garnered continual honors, including numerous solo exhibitions and publication in major national journals. Koike was imprisoned at the Minidoka Relocation Center in Idaho during World War II and never recovered his health, dying shortly after his release.

HOWARD KOTTLER originally trained as an optometrist, but a ceramics course in 1952 shifted his focus. He went on to receive a master of arts in ceramics from Ohio State University in 1956 and a master of fine arts from Cranbrook Academy of Art in Michigan in 1957. A Fulbright Fellowship allowed him to continue his studies in Finland at the Central School of Arts and Crafts and the Arabia ceramics factory. Kottler returned to Ohio State University and completed his PhD in 1964. The following year he joined the faculty at the University of Washington, where he taught for the next 24 years while pursuing an artistic career that earned him international critical acclaim. Tacoma Art Museum has held several one-person exhibitions of Kottler's work, the first in 1979; the second, *Look Alikes: The Decal Plates of Howard Kottler*, began its national tour in Tacoma in 2004. In 2010 the museum installed the two-year exhibition *Howard Kottler: A Retrospective Look*.

FRANK ASAKICHI KUNISHIGE immigrated to San Francisco in 1896. He studied at the Effingham College of Photography in Illinois in the early 1910s, returning to San Francisco to open a studio. In 1917 he moved to Seattle and worked first for photographer Edward S. Curtis (1868–1952) and then for Ella McBride (1862–1965). He also performed commissions for clients such as the Cornish School of Allied Arts (now Cornish College of the Arts), the Art Institute of Seattle, and the Bon Marché department store. Kunishige began showing his works regionally and nationally around 1919, quickly gaining international prominence. During the 1920s he was one of the most exhibited pictorialist photographers in the world. Kunishige was also one of the founding members of the Seattle Camera Club.

JAMES LAVADOUR is a self-taught painter who has exhibited frequently in the Northwest and around the United States, including one-person exhibitions at Portland Art Museum, Seattle Art Museum, the Northwest Museum of Arts and Culture in Spokane, the Maryhill Museum of Art in Goldendale, Washington, and the Eiteljorg Museum of American Indians and Western Art in Indianapolis. He received the Flintridge Foundation Award for Visual Artists in 2004 and an Honorary Doctorate of Human Letters from Eastern Oregon University in 1999. In addition to his distinguished career as an artist, Lavadour founded the Crow's Shadow Institute for the Arts in Pendleton, Oregon, in 1992 and is past president and current board member of the institute.

JACOB LAWRENCE is one of the Northwest's most celebrated artists. He began studying art as a teenager at the Harlem Community Art Center, securing a scholarship to the American Artists School in New York through the help of one of his teachers. He later worked as a painter for the Works Progress Administration's Federal Art Project. Lawrence began painting the first of his narrative series on important figures in African American history in the 1930s. His best-known series, *The Migration of the Negro*, was completed in 1941. In 1970 Lawrence became an art professor at the University of Washington. A major retrospective of his international career was organized in 2001 by The Phillips Collection, Washington, DC, and traveled to five additional venues, including Seattle Art Museum.

ISAAC LAYMAN earned a bachelor of fine arts at the University of Washington in 2003. His work has been included in one-person and group exhibitions in Seattle at Crawl Space, SOIL, the Photographic Center Northwest, and the Lawrimore Project and in Portland at the Pulliam Deffenbaugh Gallery. His work has been reviewed in *Art in America*, the *Stranger*, and the *Seattle Post-Intelligencer*. He was selected for the National Photography Competition at the Soho Photo Gallery in New York and was the winner of the 2008 Betty Bowen Memorial Award.

KEITH LEWIS received his bachelor of science in chemistry from Dickinson College in Pennsylvania in 1981 and his master of fine arts in jewelry and metalsmithing from Kent State University in Ohio in 1993. He is a professor of jewelry and metalsmithing at Central Washington University, Ellensburg, where he has taught since 1994. He has exhibited widely both nationally and internationally and his work can be found in numerous collections, including the Museum of Fine Arts in Houston, the Metropolitan Museum of Art in New York, and the Smithsonian American Art Museum in Washington, DC, as well as in regional public, private, and museum collections. He also writes for several art publications, including *Metalsmith* and *Artweek*.

WALTER LIEBERMAN received his bachelor of fine arts from Massachusetts College of Art in Boston in 1978. He has had a number of solo exhibitions in New York, San Francisco, Seattle, and Detroit. He has been a visiting artist at Pilchuck Glass School in Stanwood, Washington, and Penland School of Crafts in North Carolina, as well as teaching workshops at universities in Europe, Canada, and the United States. Lieberman's work can be found in the collections of the Corning Museum of Glass, New York; the City of Seattle; the Washington State Arts Commission; and Glasmuseum in Frauenau, Germany, in addition to private and corporate collections.

NORMAN LUNDIN studied at the School of the Art Institute of Chicago before earning his master of fine arts at the University of Cincinnati in 1963. Shortly after graduation, he began teaching at the University of Washington, where he is now professor emeritus. Lundin's work has an extensive exhibition history, including at museums and galleries in Los Angeles, Seattle, and New York, among others. His paintings can be found in the collections of the Art Institute of Chicago, the Corcoran Gallery of Art in Washington, DC, and the Museum of Modern Art in New York, as well as in numerous regional museums and corporate collections. He has received fellowships and grants from the Ford Foundation, National Endowment for the Arts, and Louis Comfort Tiffany Foundation.

DANTE MARIONI studied glassblowing at Seattle's Glass Eye Studio and with artists such as Lino Tagliapietra (born 1934), Richard Marquis (born 1945), and Benjamin Moore (born 1952) at Pilchuck Glass School in Stanwood, Washington. He has had one-person exhibitions at the Museum of Glass, Tacoma; the Museum of Northwest Art, La Conner; the Amarillo Museum of Art, Texas; and the Muskegon Museum of Art, Michigan. His work also has been included in numerous group exhibitions. His awards include a Louis Comfort Tiffany Foundation Award in 1987 and the Outstanding Achievement in Glass Award from Urban-Glass, New York City, in 1997. His work is the subject of the book *Dante Marioni: Blown Glass,* and his glass objects are included in the permanent collections of more than 20 museums worldwide.

PAUL MARIONI is known as an innovator in the glass world. He studied at San Francisco State University and then received his bachelor of arts from the University of Cincinnati in 1967. He has exhibited extensively in the Northwest as well as in California, Virginia, Massachusetts, New York, and Darmstadt, Germany. He has received numerous awards, including a lifetime achievement award from the Glass Art Society in 2004, several fellowships from the National Endowment for the Arts, and the John H. Hauberg Fellowship at Pilchuck Glass School. His work can be found in the collections of the Corning Glass Museum in Corning, New York, the American Craft Museum (now the Museum of Arts and Design) in New York City, the Hessisches Landesmuseum in Darmstadt, Germany, and in numerous regional collections. He taught at Pilchuck Glass School in Stanwood, Washington from 1974 through 1988.

SHERRY MARKOVITZ received her bachelor of arts from the University of Wisconsin, Madison, in 1969 and her master of fine arts in printmaking from the University of Washington in 1975. Her mixed-media works are featured in numerous public and private collections, including the Corning Glass Museum, Corning, New York; the American Craft Museum (now the Museum of Arts and Design), New York City; Seattle Art Museum; the Seattle City Light 1% for Art Collection; and Microsoft Corporation, among others. Her work was the subject of a midcareer retrospective in 2008 at Bellevue Arts Museum, *Sherry Markovitz: Shimmer, Paintings and Sculptures 1979–2007.*

ALDEN MASON graduated from the University of Washington in 1947 with his master of fine arts and joined the School of Art faculty later the same year, teaching until his retirement in 1981. Mason taught generations of art students, notably Chuck Close (born 1940), who in turn introduced Mason to the New York art world. His works have been shown in more than 100 exhibitions and can be found in museum collections such as the Henry Art Gallery at the University of Washington, Seattle Art Museum, the San Francisco Museum of Modern Art, and Milwaukee Art Museum as well as in many private and corporate collections.

ELLA MCBRIDE was highly successful and internationally known though her photographic career was brief. Starting in 1889 she worked as a school teacher and principal in Portland, Oregon, before becoming manager in 1907 of the Seattle studio of photographer Edward S. Curtis (1868–1952), whom she met climbing Mount Rainier. McBride ran Curtis's studio for eight years before opening her own in 1916 with photographer Wayne Albee (1882–1937). Her assistants included Frank Kunishige (1878–1960) and Soichi Sunami (1885–1971), who both went on to internationally successful photographic careers. In addition to her studio work, she provided illustrations for Seattle's *Town Crier* as well as other regional publications.

MATT MCCORMICK is an Oregon filmmaker and photographer. He has had three films screen at the Sundance Film Festival and has had work screened or exhibited at the Museum of Modern Art in New York, the Serpentine Gallery in London, the Oslo Museum of Modern Art, Reykjavik Art Museum, and Seattle Art Museum. In 2007 he was selected to participate in both the Moscow Biennial and Art Basel. He has received several awards, including Best Short Film from the San Francisco International Film Fest, Best Experimental Film from the New York Underground Film Fest, and Best Narrative from the Ann Arbor Film Fest. His film *The Subconscious Art of Graffiti Removal* was named one of the *Village Voice*'s Top 10 Avant Garde Films of 2002 and one of the Best of 2002 in *Artforum* magazine.

NANCY MEE received her bachelor of fine arts in printmaking from the University of Washington in 1974 after study at the American Center for Art and Culture and Atelier 17 in Paris. She began working in glass in the early 1980s, including a residency at Pilchuck Glass School in Stanwood, Washington in 1984. Mee's work has been included in numerous exhibitions both regionally and nationally and can be found in public and private collections, including those of the Microsoft Corporation, Seattle Art Museum, and the Musée des Arts Decoratives, Lausanne, Switzerland, among others. She also has created a number of public art commissions for institutions such as the Swedish Medical Center in Seattle, the University of Oregon Library in Eugene, and the Washington Center for the Performing Arts in Olympia.

MARK TAKAMICHI MILLER studied psychology and art at the University of California, Santa Cruz, and earned his master of fine arts from the University of Iowa in 1991. He has had one-person exhibitions at the King County Arts Commission Gallery, Seattle, and the Laverne Krause Gallery at the University of Oregon. He has shown extensively throughout the United States and the Puget Sound region, including at the Northwest Annual, Bumbershoot Arts Festival, and *LAVA 2002*. He has taught as a visiting artist at the University of Washington and the University of Oregon, among others. His work is included in the City of Seattle Portable Works Collection and the Microsoft Art Collection. He has received two fellowships from the MacDowell Colony and was awarded a Neddy Artist Fellowship in 2001.

JEFFRY MITCHELL has received critical acclaim for his mastery of painting, printmaking, sculpture, installation, and ceramics. He earned his master of fine arts in printmaking from Temple University, Philadelphia, in 1988. He has had one-person exhibitions at the Henry Art Gallery, University of Washington; Seattle Art Museum; and the New Museum, New York. Mitchell has been artist in residence at Pilchuck Glass School, Rhode Island School of Design, and Harvard University, and he has taught art at the Emily Carr University of Art + Design in British Columbia, the University of Washington, and Cornish College of the Arts. His work has been included in exhibitions at Portland Art Museum and the Philadelphia Museum of Art and was the subject of a retrospective exhibition at the Henry Art Gallery in 2012.

YUKIO MORINAGA immigrated to the United States in the early 1900s, arriving in Seattle in 1907. He worked in the camera department of a local drug store, where he met several other Japanese photography enthusiasts; together they encouraged each other's work, eventually founding the Seattle Camera Club. Morinaga began exhibiting work at the Frederick and Nelson Salons in Seattle in 1924 and went on to exhibit his work in national and international photography salons. Through the Seattle Camera Club he met Tacoma photographer Virna Haffer (1899–1974), and they began a lifelong friendship and artistic collaboration. Morinaga became Haffer's assistant, developing and printing the majority of her works, a relationship that continued until his imprisonment at the Minidoka Relocation Center, Idaho, during World War II. Although Morinaga produced hundreds of exhibition prints during his lifetime, only about 30 of his photographs have survived, through the efforts of Haffer and her descendants.

CARL MORRIS was one of the most distinguished Oregon painters. He trained at the School of the Art Institute of Chicago and in Paris and Vienna. After teaching at the San Francisco Art Institute, he was invited in 1938 to run the Spokane Art Center under the Federal Art Project. In the early 1940s he moved to Oregon with his wife, the sculptor Hilda Morris (1911–1991). During his career Morris received numerous awards, including the Austro-American Scholarship, the Werkbund Scholarship, and Seattle Art Museum's Margaret E. Fuller Award. His works were featured in one-person and group exhibitions worldwide, including at the Fondation des Etats-Unis in Paris, Seattle Art Museum, the Art Institute of Chicago, and the São Paulo (Brazil) Biennial Exhibition.

HILDA MORRIS began her formal studies at Cooper Union and later trained at the Art Students League in New York. In 1938 she was invited to organize a sculpture program for the Federal Art Center in Spokane. In 1940 she moved to Portland with her husband, the painter Carl Morris (1911–1993), and taught briefly at the Museum Art School of the Portland Art Museum (now the Pacific Northwest College of Art). A native of New York City, during the course of her career she exhibited in New York, San Francisco, Seattle, and Portland and created a number of public and private sculptures for sites throughout the Northwest, particularly in Seattle, Portland, and Eugene, Oregon. In 1985 she was the recipient of a Ford Foundation grant and the Oregon Governor's Arts Award. Her work was the subject of a major retrospective and catalogue at Portland Art Museum in 2006.

WILLIAM MORRIS is an internationally known glass artist and is considered an innovator in the field, particularly in his treatments of surface texture. He was educated at California State University in Chico and at Central Washington University in Ellensburg. Early in his career he was a gaffer (master glassblower) for Dale Chihuly (born 1941). He then went on to maintain his own studio. His glass sculptures are part of the permanent collections of many museums, including the Metropolitan Museum of Art and the Museum of Arts and Design in New York, the Chrysler Museum of Art in Norfolk, Virginia, the Louvre in Paris, the Victoria and Albert Museum in London, and the Musée des Arts Décoratifs in Paris.

SPENCER MOSELEY was a pivotal figure in the Washington art scene. He taught for 26 years at the University of Washington, also serving as director of the School of Art and acting director of the Henry Art Gallery. In addition, as a dedicated advocate for Northwest art he wrote a number of publications on Northwest artists. Moseley trained at the University of Washington and then with the legendary modernist Fernand Léger (1881–1955) in Paris. Though he created a large body of paintings and prints, he rarely exhibited or sold his work.

ROBERT MOTHERWELL was one of the leading figures in the abstract expressionist movement. He studied philosophy at Stanford and Harvard Universities before studying art and art history at Columbia University in New York, where he quickly became associated with the group of young artists known as the New York school, or the abstract expressionists. In 1944 Motherwell had his first one-person show at Peggy Guggenheim's influential gallery, Art of This Century, and his career rapidly blossomed from that point on. He became an internationally respected painter, writer, lecturer, and teacher. In 1965 his work was the subject of a major retrospective exhibition at the Museum of Modern Art, followed by numerous retrospectives in Europe and the United States over the next few decades. His works can be found in the collections of major museums throughout the world.

MARK MUMFORD received his bachelor of arts degree from Kenyon College in Ohio in 1981. He has had solo exhibitions at numerous Seattle galleries and in Portland, Oregon. His work has been included in regional group exhibitions, including *Baja to Vancouver: The West Coast and Contemporary Art* in 2003, which traveled to Seattle, San Diego, San Francisco, and Vancouver, British Columbia. He also has exhibited work in Arizona and Ohio. Mumford has received numerous grants and awards, including a MacDowell Fellowship in 1988, a Yaddo Artist Residency in 1990, and a GAP Grant from Artist Trust in 2001.

KENJIRO NOMURA immigrated to the United States in 1907 and became a well-respected and prolific Northwest artist. His solo exhibition was one of the first shows at Seattle Art Museum when it opened in 1933, and he also exhibited work at such prestigious venues as the Palace of the Legion of Honor in San Francisco and the Museum of Modern Art in New York. During World War II he was imprisoned with other Japanese Americans at the Minidoka Relocation Center in Idaho. He continued to paint, using whatever materials he could scavenge to create images of life in the camps. After the war he returned to Seattle and resumed his professional career. His work was the subject of a nationally touring exhibition in the 1990s and a 2012 exhibition at the Seattle Asian Art Museum.

FRANK OKADA received his bachelor of fine arts from Cranbrook Academy of Art, Bloomfield, Michigan, in 1957 and went on to receive Whitney, Guggenheim, and Fulbright Fellowships after graduation. He began teaching at the University of Oregon in 1969, where he worked until his death in 2000. His work can be found in corporate and museum collections throughout the Northwest, including Seattle Art Museum, Portland Art Museum, and the Jordan Schnitzer Museum of Art in Eugene, Oregon. His work was the focus of solo exhibitions at the Whatcom Museum of Art (now the Whatcom Museum) in Bellingham, Portland Art Museum, and Cornish College of the Arts in Seattle, among others; the Museum of Northwest Art in La Conner held a posthumous retrospective of his work in 2005.

MARVIN OLIVER is an internationally renowned carver, glass artist, printmaker, and teacher. He has worked in a variety of media, including cedar, bronze, steel, and glass, and has created both smaller-scale and monumental works for public settings in the United States, Canada, Japan, and Italy. He is professor of American Indian studies and art at the University of Washington, where he also serves as adjunct curator of contemporary Native American art at the Burke Museum of Natural History and

Culture. He also holds a part-time post at the University of Alaska, Ketchikan.

JOSEPH PARK earned a master of fine arts in 1988 from the California Institute of the Arts in Valencia and a bachelor of applied arts in 1990 from Cornish College of the Arts in Seattle. In 2005 Park was featured in the one-person exhibition *Moon Beam Caress* at Frye Art Museum, Seattle, and was awarded the Neddy Artist Fellowship in Painting that same year. His paintings have been included in group exhibitions at Seattle Art Museum; the Art Gym at Marylhurst University, Portland, Oregon; the Regina Gouger Miller Gallery at Carnegie Mellon University, Pittsburgh, Pennsylvania; the Henry Art Gallery, University of Washington; and the Gwangju Biennale in South Korea. His paintings are in numerous private collections in Seattle as well as Seattle Art Museum.

LUCINDA PARKER earned a master of fine arts degree from Pratt Institute, Brooklyn, in 1968 and then returned to Portland, Oregon, where she began teaching at the Pacific Northwest College of Art in 1972, a position she held until 2006. She also has taught at universities in Oregon, California, and Washington. Her paintings can be found in numerous corporate, private, and museum collections across the Northwest. She also has executed commissions for a number of public buildings, including the federal courthouse in Bakersfield, California; the Ford Alumni Center, University of Oregon; and City Hall, Portland, Oregon. Her extensive exhibition history includes one-person exhibitions at Pacific Northwest College of Art, Boise Art Museum, and Seattle Art Museum and a retrospective at Portland Art Museum in 1995.

CAMILLE PATHA received her bachelor of arts and master of fine arts degrees from the University of Washington, in 1960 and 1965, respectively. In 1970 she was invited to participate in the Washington State delegation to the Osaka World's Fair, an event that brought her work to greater public attention. A prolific artist, her work can be found in numerous museum collections, including Seattle Art Museum and Jundt Art Museum, Spokane, as well as in public collections across Washington State.

AMBROSE PATTERSON, born in Australia, studied art in Paris and assembled an impressive exhibition history at the Paris Salon d'Automne, the Royal Academy in London, and the Guggenheim Museum in New York, among others. He relocated to Hawaii in 1916 and then San Francisco, arriving in the Northwest in 1918. He founded the School of Painting and Design at the University of Washington (now the School of Art) and was one of the first modernist artists to bring a range of avant-garde artistic ideas to the region. Seattle Art Museum held three solo exhibitions of his work in the 1930s to 1950s as well as a retrospective in 1961.

RUTH PENINGTON was a prominent Northwest jeweler who influenced generations of students and helped foster the studio art jewelry movement in the Northwest. She received her bachelor of fine arts in 1927 and her master of fine arts in 1929, both from the University of Washington. She then began teaching at the University of Washington, becoming a full professor in 1951 and continuing until 1969. Penington also helped found the Northwest Designer Craftsmen in 1954. The Henry Art Gallery held retrospectives of her work in 1962 and on her retirement in 1969.

MARY ANN PETERS earned a bachelor of arts in 1971 from the University of California, Santa Barbara, and a master of fine arts in 1977 from the University of Washington. She has exhibited extensively throughout the region in both solo and group exhibitions, and her work can be found in numerous regional collections. She won the Neddy Artist Fellowship in 2000 and received a second nomination for this award in 2005.

SHAUN PETERSON (QWALSIUS), began sketching at a young age and began working as a sculptor shortly after graduating from high school. He received his training from Native master carvers, including Steve Brown, Greg Colfax, and Loren White. He also paints and creates screen prints. His work has been exhibited in Washington and in Victoria, British Columbia. In the fall of 2005 Peterson received the Native name Qwalsius, which belonged to his great-grandfather. With Peterson's acceptance of the name, his work becomes a personal expression but also honors his immediate family, the community of which he is a part, and his people's ancestors.

MARY RANDLETT has lived her entire life in the Puget Sound area. She taught herself photography, working in the chemistry building's darkroom at Whitman College in Walla Walla and apprenticing briefly with photographer Hans Jorgensen (1915–2003). Her work is in the collection of more than 40 American museums, including Seattle Art Museum, the Metropolitan Museum of Art in New York, and the National Portrait Gallery of the Smithsonian Institution in Washington, DC; and her work appears in more than 200 books and exhibition catalogues. She has received numerous grants, awards, and citations, including a National Endowment for the Arts Fellowship and, in 1983, a Washington State Governor's Award of Special Commendation for "unique contributions to the field."

VANESSA RENWICK is an Oregon photographer, filmmaker, and installation artist. She has exhibited her work at museums, galleries, and film festivals throughout the United States and internationally, including shows in the Netherlands, Belgium, Germany, Turkey, Spain, and England. Her videos and installations reflect her interests in places and borders, the relationships between people and the natural world, and how the body physically experiences emotion and memory. *Mighty Tacoma* was screened at the Centre Pompidou in Paris in 2011.

SUSAN ROBB earned both a bachelor of fine arts and a bachelor of arts from Syracuse University and completed her master of fine arts at the University of Washington. She has had one-person exhibitions at the Henry Art Gallery, University of Washington, and at Consolidated Works, the Platform Gallery, and the Lawrimore Project, also in Seattle. Her work was included in the exhibition *Gene(sis): Contemporary Art Explores Human Genomics*, organized by the Henry Art Gallery, as well as in Tacoma Art Museum's *9th Northwest Biennial*. She is the recipient of a Pollock-Krasner Foundation grant as well as grants from 4Culture, the City of Seattle, and Artist Trust.

BARBARA ROBERTSON earned a master of fine arts from the University of Washington in 1979. She is a board member, past president, and cofounder of Seattle Print Arts, an organization that fosters and expands knowledge and appreciation of print arts. She also has served on the Board of Trustees for Pratt Fine Arts Center, Seattle. Robertson has exhibited her prints throughout the Northwest and in group exhibitions in China, Canada, Mexico, Cuba, and England. She has received grants from the Kala Art Institute in Berkeley, Washington State Arts Commission, City of Seattle, and King County Arts Commission. Her work is included in the collections of 4Culture Portable Works, City of Seattle, and the State of Washington. Since 2009 she has begun experimenting with combinations of print and digital media.

MICHELE RUSSO received his bachelor of fine arts from Yale University in 1934. He moved to Portland, Oregon, in 1947 to teach at the Museum Art School of the Portland Art Museum (now the Pacific Northwest College of Art), where he worked for 27 years, mentoring generations of Northwest art students. His extensive exhibition history includes the Seattle World's Fair in 1962, *Art of the Pacific Northwest* at the Smithsonian Institution in 1974, the Corcoran Gallery of Art Biennial in 1983, in Washington, DC, and *Michele Russo: A Fifty Year Retrospective* at Portland Art Museum in 1988. Honors received include the Oregon Governor's Arts Award and Portland's Metropolitan Arts Commission Award. He also cofounded the seminal contemporary arts organization Portland Center for the Visual Arts in 1973.

NORIE SATO graduated with a bachelor of fine arts from the University of Michigan in 1971 and a master of fine arts from the University of Washington in 1974. Since 1982 she has completed a number of public art commissions, including for transit projects in Seattle, Phoenix, Portland (Oregon), and Salt Lake City, as well as installations at the Dallas Convention Center and Portland City Hall. She has had more than 15 solo exhibitions across the United States and has received several awards, including the Artist Trust Media Arts Fellowship and an Artist Fellowship from the Washington State Arts Commission for her video-related works. She also has received the Betty Bowen Memorial Award and three National Endowment for the Arts Fellowships.

ALEX SCHWEDER earned a bachelor of architecture from Pratt Institute, Brooklyn, in 1993 and a master of architecture from Princeton University in 1998. He was the 2005 fellow in architecture at the American Academy in Rome, and he was the 2009 artist in residence at the Chinati Foundation in Marfa, Texas. He has been featured in the publications *Modern Painters, Artforum,* and the *New York Times.* Some of the significant moments of his career occurred in Tacoma, including a major commission, *Lovelorn Walls,* at the Tacoma Trade and Convention Center and *Melting Instructions* at Tacoma Art Museum.

SUSAN SEUBERT graduated from the Pacific Northwest College of Art, Portland, Oregon, with a bachelor of fine arts in photography. She has had one-person exhibitions at galleries in Portland, Seattle, and Houston, and her work has been included in group exhibitions at Frye Art Museum in Seattle, the Art Gym at Marylhurst University in Portland, Portland Art Museum, and *The 9th Northwest Biennial* at Tacoma Art Museum. Her work is in several museum collections, including Portland Art Museum, the Museum of Fine Arts in Houston, and the Hallie Ford Museum of Art in Salem, Oregon. Her work has been reviewed in the *Oregonian,* the *New York Times, Camera Arts Magazine,* and the *Seattle Times.*

ROGER SHIMOMURA received a bachelor of arts from the University of Washington in 1961 and a master of fine arts from Syracuse University, New York, in 1969. He has had more than 125 solo exhibitions and has presented his experimental theater pieces at such venues as the Franklin Furnace, New York City; Walker Art Center, Minneapolis; and the Smithsonian Institution, Washington, DC. He has been the recipient of numerous grants and awards and has lectured on his work at universities and museums across the country. He taught at the University of Kansas, Lawrence, for 35 years before retiring in 2004.

JEFFREY SIMMONS graduated with a bachelor of fine arts from the School of Art, University of Michigan, Ann Arbor, in 1991. In 1996 he received both a Betty Bowen Committee Special Recognition Award and a Pilloff Scholarship from Pilchuck Glass School in Stanwood, Washington. In 2005 he was nominated for the Neddy Artist Fellowship in Painting. His work can be found in numerous corporate and public collections in the Puget Sound region and has been exhibited in Portland, Tacoma, Seattle, and Michigan. In 2001 the Whatcom County Museum of Art, Bellingham (now the Whatcom Museum), held a solo exhibition of his work.

PRESTON SINGLETARY learned to work with glass by assisting artists such as Dante Marioni (born 1964) and Benjamin Moore (born 1952) and alongside masters of the Venetian tradition of glassmaking, including Lino Tagliapietra (born 1934) and Pino Signoretto (born 1944). He also traveled to Sweden to study Scandinavian design at Kosta Boda. He credits his mentor, Northwest Coast artist Joe David (born 1946), with helping him better express his own Native heritage through his work. Singletary's sculptures can be found in museum collections in Stockholm, Boston, Corning (New York), and Seattle, among others. He also teaches and lectures internationally. In 2009 the Museum of Glass, Tacoma, held a midcareer survey of his work.

KIFF SLEMMONS received a bachelor of arts in art and French from the University of Iowa in 1968. Self-taught as a metalsmith, she began making jewelry in the 1970s. Her work has been exhibited nationally and internationally, including a midcareer retrospective at the Palo Alto Art Center, California, in 2000. Her work can be found in numerous museum collections, including the Victoria and Albert Museum, London; the Metropolitan Museum of Art and the Museum of Arts and Design, New York; the Mint Museum, North Carolina; and the Museum of Fine Arts, Boston. Since 2000 she has been collaborating with artisans at Arte Papel in Oaxaca, Mexico, to create paper jewelry using indigenous plants and fibers.

RAMONA SOLBERG studied at the University of Washington with jewelers Coralyn Pence (1909–1994) and Ruth Penington (1905–1998) as well as in Mexico. She taught at Central Washington State College (now Central Washington University) in Ellensburg and was associate professor of art at the University of Washington from 1956 to 1967. Solberg was a pioneer in the contemporary jewelry movement, particularly in the use of found objects and ethnic items acquired during her travels. She also often used forged and fabricated metals. Her work can be found in the collections of the Renwick Gallery, Smithsonian American Art Museum, and of the Museum of Arts and Design, New York, among others.

MICHAEL SPAFFORD received his master of arts from Harvard University in 1960, after which he relocated to Seattle to teach painting at the University of Washington. He also was a fellow at the American Academy in Rome from 1967 through 1969. Spafford has had many solo exhibitions at Northwest institutions, including the Hallie Ford Museum of Art (Salem, Oregon), Bellevue Arts Museum, Seattle Art Museum, and Tacoma Art Museum. His work is included in the Microsoft Art Collection, Washington State Art Collection, and the City of Seattle Portable Works Collection as well as in Seattle Art Museum. He has received commissions for public works from the Seattle Opera House, King County, and the State of Washington. Spafford was included in *The 8th Northwest Biennial* at Tacoma Art Museum in 2007.

JULIE SPEIDEL studied at the University of Washington, Cornish College of the Arts, and the University of Grenoble in France. She has had solo exhibitions in Seattle, New York, California, and Idaho and has participated in numerous group exhibitions and sculpture invitationals. She has created a number of site-specific works in the Northwest, including for Central Oregon Community College in Bend, the University of Washington, the Federal Courthouse in

Seattle, the Puget Sound Energy building in Bellevue, and Nordstrom Corporation. Her work is also part of the United States Art in Embassies program.

PEGGY STRONG was a Tacoma artist who made her reputation painting realist images and murals. She studied at the University of Washington and with painters Alice Engley Beek (1867–1951) and Mark Tobey (1890–1976), among others. Despite a traumatic injury in 1933, she continued to paint. A member of the Women Painters of Washington, Strong exhibited regionally in Seattle, Portland, and San Francisco as well as nationally, including at the Museum of Modern Art in New York. She worked briefly in San Francisco before her untimely death at 44.

AKIO TAKAMORI earned a master of fine arts in ceramics at Alfred University in New York in 1978. His exhibition history includes a midcareer survey, *Between Clouds of Memory,* organized by Arizona State University Art Museum. The exhibition traveled to Tacoma Art Museum, the Art Gym at Marylhurst University in Portland, Oregon, and Racine Art Museum in Wisconsin. Additionally, his work has been featured in one-person exhibitions at the Tempe Center for the Arts in Arizona and European Ceramic Work Centre in the Netherlands. His work is in national and international collections, including the Victoria and Albert Museum in London, Taipei Fine Arts Museum in Taiwan, the Museum of Contemporary Ceramic Art in Japan, the Archie Bray Foundation for the Ceramic Arts in Helena, Montana, and local public, corporate, and museum collections. His work has been included in many books and reviewed in *Ceramics Monthly, Artnews, Sculpture,* and the *New York Times.*

LORI TALCOTT earned her bachelor of arts in humanities at Lund University, Sweden, in 1983 and her bachelor of fine arts in metal design at the University of Washington in 1990. From 1990 to 1991, she apprenticed with a Norwegian master silversmith. Talcott was awarded Artist Trust fellowships in 1997 and 2006 and a fellowship from the American-Scandinavian Foundation in 2004. Her work has been exhibited nationally and in Europe and can be found in numerous private and museum collections, including the Renwick Gallery, Smithsonian American Art Museum. Her work has been featured in *Metalsmith, Ornament, Korean Craft,* and various other publications.

WHITING TENNIS graduated from the University of Washington in 1984 with a bachelor of fine arts. His work has been included in group exhibitions throughout the Northwest and in Chicago, San Francisco, New York, and Boston. Tennis has had one-person gallery exhibitions in New York, Portland, and Seattle and most recently at the Frances Young Tang Teaching Museum and Art Gallery, Skidmore College, in 2011. He received a Pollock-Krasner Foundation grant in 1993 and the Arlene Schnitzer Prize in association with the Contemporary Northwest Art Awards exhibition at Portland Art Museum, Oregon, in 2008.

BARBARA EARL THOMAS is an artist, writer, arts administrator, and currently the executive director of the Northwest African American Museum in Seattle. She studied painting with Jacob Lawrence (1917–2000) at the University of Washington, earning both her bachelor and master of fine arts degrees. She has exhibited work at Seattle Art Museum, the Whatcom Museum of History and Art (now the Whatcom Museum) in Bellingham, and Tacoma Art Museum as well as in a nationally touring exhibition.

CAPPY THOMPSON received her bachelor of arts in 1976 from The Evergreen State College, Olympia, in painting and printmaking; she began working with glass in 1975. Thompson has taught at Pilchuck Glass School in Stanwood, Washington and Penland School of Crafts in North Carolina. She has exhibited her work across the United States and in British Columbia and Japan, including as part of the Smithsonian Institution's traveling exhibition *American Glass: Masters of the Art,* from 1998 to 2000, and *Contemporary Directions: Glass from the Maxine and William Block Collection* at the Carnegie Museum of Art, Pittsburgh, in 2002. Her work can be found in numerous collections, including the Corning Glass Museum, Corning, New York; the American Craft Museum (now the Museum of Arts and Design), New York City; the Art Gallery of Western Australia, Perth; and the Hokkaido Museum of Modern Art, Japan. She also has created a number of site-specific installations around Seattle.

MARK TOBEY studied at the School of the Art Institute of Chicago from 1906 to 1908 and then moved to New York, where he worked as a fashion illustrator for *McCall's* magazine. He had his first solo show at M. Knoedler & Co., New York, in 1917. In 1922 Tobey moved to Seattle to teach at the progressive Cornish School of Allied Arts (now Cornish College of the Arts). He began traveling worldwide during this period, a habit that became lifelong. From 1931 to 1938 he taught at Dartington Hall in Devonshire, England, returning to Seattle just before World War II. Here he became friends with Morris Graves (1910–2001), Kenneth Callahan (1905–1986), and Guy Anderson (1906–1998), a group that collectively became known as the Northwest Mystics for their shared aesthetics. Tobey became nationally and internationally successful with solo exhibitions in San Francisco, New York, and Paris, among others. In 1958 he became the first American since James Abbott McNeill Whistler (1834–1903) to receive the first prize for painting at the Venice Biennale.

TERRY TOEDTEMEIER received a bachelor's degree in earth sciences from Oregon State University in 1969. A self-taught photographer, he played a vital role in the evolution of photography in the Northwest through his own work; his role as the first curator of photography at Portland Art Museum; as a cofounder of the artist-run Blue Sky Gallery, Portland, in 1975; and as a photo historian. Among the many honors Toedtemeier received were two National Endowment for the Arts Fellowships and a Flintridge Foundation Award for Visual Artists. His work is in many prestigious museum collections, including the Smithsonian American Art Museum and the San Francisco Museum of Modern Art.

MARGARET TOMKINS earned both her bachelor of fine arts and master of fine arts at the University of California, Los Angeles, in the 1930s. She arrived in Seattle in 1939, where she taught for several brief periods at the University of Washington. She also taught for a short time at the Spokane Art Center. She had her first solo exhibition in 1941 at Seattle Art Museum. As early as 1939 her work began to be included in national exhibitions, and she went on to participate in numerous exhibits regionally as well as at such prestigious institutions as the Smithsonian Institution in Washington, DC, the Whitney Museum of American Art and the Metropolitan Museum of Art in New York, the Art Institute of Chicago, and the Los Angeles County Museum of Art.

DON TOMPKINS began his studies with jeweler Russell Day (born 1912) at Everett High School, later becoming his studio assistant at Everett Junior College. Tompkins went on to earn a bachelor of arts in 1956 and a master's certificate in 1958 from the University of Washington; he also pursued graduate studies at Syracuse University and Columbia Teachers College, New York. He taught for several years at Everett Junior College and then accepted a position teaching jewelry at Central Washington State College (now Central Washington University) in Ellensburg, where he stayed for five years. Subsequent teaching appointments included the University of Washington and New York University. Tompkins worked and showed his jewelry throughout his lifetime, winning a number of awards and creating a small but innovative and influential body of work.

GEORGE TSUTAKAWA studied art at the University of Washington from 1932 to 1937. After serving in the US Army as a Japanese language instructor, he completed his master of fine arts in 1950. Tsutakawa taught at the University of Washington from 1947 to 1976 and influenced a number of local artists, including Mark Tobey (1890–1976) and Morris Graves (1910–2001). He created nearly 60 public fountains, including one for the cloister of the National Cathedral in Washington, DC, in 1968. In 1981 Tsutakawa received the Order of the Rising Sun Award, Fourth Class, from the emperor of Japan. His work was the subject of the exhibition *Eternal Laughter: A Sixty-Year Retrospective* at Bellevue Art Museum (now Bellevue Arts Museum) in 1990.

JULIUS TWOHY was born on the Ute Reservation in Utah. He was primarily self-taught as an artist, at first working in oil and watercolor and later turning to wood carving. Twohy lived in Seattle in the 1930s and 1940s and was mentored and championed by the artist Mark Tobey (1890–1976). In the late 1930s he was hired by the Works Progress Administration's Federal Art Project to paint a mural for the Cushman Indian Hospital on the Puyallup Indian Reservation; he also produced a number of lithographs for the Washington project. Little is currently known about his career after he left Washington.

MERRILL WAGNER, originally from the Northwest, received her bachelor of arts from Sarah Lawrence College in 1957, followed by several years of further study at the Art Students League, New York. During the 1960s she began working in a minimalist abstract style that she has continued to explore throughout her career. Wagner's work has been included in more than 40 individual and group exhibitions in the United States and abroad, and her work is in both public and private collections in Europe and the United States. She also has self-published five books, including *A Calendar* (1983), *Notes on Paint* (1990), and *Time and Materials* (1995). Wagner received a National Endowment for the Arts Visual Artists Fellowship grant in 1989 and the Andrew Carnegie Prize from the National Academy of Design in 2006, among other honors.

PATTI WARASHINA received her bachelor of fine arts in 1962 and her master of fine arts in 1964, both from the University of Washington, where she has taught for more than 25 years. She has shown at museums and galleries across the United States, including a retrospective at Bellevue Art Museum (now Bellevue Arts Museum) in 1991. Warashina received the Twining Humber Award for Lifetime Artistic Achievement from Artist Trust in 2002, and has received grants from the National Endowment for the Arts in 1975 and 1986. Her work is in numerous museum collections in the United States and abroad, including the Museum of Arts and Design in New York; the Smithsonian American Art Museum in Washington, DC; the Icheon World Ceramic Center in South Korea; and the Kyoto National Museum of Modern Art, among others.

JAMES WASHINGTON JR. began drawing and painting in his early teens, teaching himself through home-study courses and careful observation of other artists' work. He later studied with the artists Mark Tobey (1890–1976) and Yvonne Twining Humber (1907–2004). His first employment as an artist was for the Federal Art Project of the Works Progress Administration in the 1930s. Washington began to exhibit regionally in the mid-1940s. During the early 1950s he began creating stone and wood sculptures, works that brought him a heightened level of recognition, including an exhibition at the M. H. de Young Memorial Museum in San Francisco in 1959, a successful international artistic career, and numerous awards and honors. His work has been shown extensively, most notably in retrospective exhibitions at Frye Art Museum in Seattle in 1980, Bellevue Art Museum (now Bellevue Arts Museum) in 1989, and the Washington State History Museum in Tacoma in 2002.

MARIE WATT began her formal education at Willamette University, Salem, Oregon, and then pursued an associate of fine arts in museum studies from the Institute of American Indian Arts, Santa Fe. She earned a master of fine arts from Yale University in

1996. She was awarded the Betty Bowen Memorial Award in 2005 and a Painters and Sculptors Grant Program Award from the Joan Mitchell Foundation in 2006, and she was artist in residence at the Fabric Workshop in Philadelphia in 2008. Watt is currently the subject of a retrospective, *Marie Watt: Lodge,* organized by the Hallie Ford Museum of Art at Willamette University and exhibited at Tacoma Art Museum.

ALICE WHEELER left home as a teenager to travel throughout the American West, eventually landing in Hollywood, where she became a part of the punk rock music scene. She moved to the Northwest in the 1980s, earning her bachelor of fine arts from The Evergreen State College in Olympia in 1988. Her images of the emerging punk and grunge music scenes in the Northwest have been published by *Rolling Stone* and other national publications and helped define this movement for a generation. Her photographs have been included in numerous exhibitions in the Northwest, including *Hereabouts: Northwest Pictures by Seven Photographers* at Seattle Art Museum and *Sparkle Then Fade* at Tacoma Art Museum. Her work also was included in *The Sounds I See: Photographs of Musicians* at the Museum of Fine Arts, Houston. She continues to work as a professional photographer, shooting assignments for magazines as well as album covers and books.

MYRA WIGGINS trained as a painter at the Art Students League in New York before deciding to pursue photography as a career. Though she always described herself as an amateur photographer, her career was highly successful. She won numerous awards and exhibited extensively both nationally and internationally. Wiggins also was a member of London's Linked Ring and New York's Photo-Secession, exclusive and pivotal early organizations in the development and promotion of photography as an art form. In the 1910s, Wiggins once again began to focus on painting, building an international reputation and coming to be known as a leading figure among the Northwest's women painters. She had one-person exhibitions in New York, Chicago, and New Orleans and helped found the Women Painters of Washington. Seattle Art Museum held a major retrospective exhibition of her paintings and photographs in 1953, followed by the M. H. de Young Memorial Museum, San Francisco, the next year.

MATIKA WILBUR studied photography at the Rocky Mountain School of Photography in Montana and the Brooks Institute of Photography in California. She has exhibited at the Royal British Columbia Museum, the Nantes Museum of Art in France, Seattle Art Museum, and the Burke Museum of Natural History and Culture at the University of Washington, as well as nationally at numerous art galleries. To date, she has created four major series of work: *We Are One People,* character study portraits of Coast Salish elders; *iHuman,* images interwoven with cedar bark; and *We Emerge,* a photographic meditation that examines stereotypical depictions of Native peoples. Her fourth and most recent series, *Save the Indian and Kill the Man,* was exhibited at Seattle Art Museum in 2011.

NANCY WORDEN studied at Central Washington State College (now Central Washington University) in Ellensburg with artist and professor Ken Cory (1943–1994), who became an important mentor and key influence on her career. Her work has received national acclaim in such publications as *Metalsmith, Ornament,* and *Craft in America.* Her works have been included in exhibitions across the United States, Europe, and Australia and can be found in the collections of the Museum of Fine Arts, Boston; the Museum of Fine Arts, Houston; the Museum of Arts and Design, New York; and the Stedelijk Museum, Amsterdam, among others. Her work was the subject of the retrospective traveling exhibition *Loud Bones: The Jewelry of Nancy Worden* at Tacoma Art Museum in 2009.

CLAUDE ZERVAS studied art at Western Washington University, Bellingham, and also trained as a software engineer. His works have been included in group exhibitions at Seattle Art Museum, Portland Art Museum, the Whatcom Museum of History and Art (now the Whatcom Museum) in Bellingham, and Western Bridge in Seattle. They are also included in the collections of the Whitney Museum of American Art, New York, and Seattle Art Museum, among others. Zervas has executed a number of public commissions around Seattle, including works for the Kenmore Branch of the King County Library and Seattle City Light.

Tacoma Art Museum Staff

Stephanie A. Stebich, Director

Kaela Arellano, Cafe Staff
Meredith Bachman, Graphic and Web Design Coordinator
Ryan Branchini, Museum Educator
Joan Budd, Development Assistant
Derrek Bull, Security Officer
Margaret Bullock, Curator of Collections and Special Exhibitions
Melinda Campbell, Store Manager
Caitlin Chaffee, Gala Manager
Adrianna Chapman, Tour Sales
Irene Conley, Security Officer
Kelly Crithfield, Assistant to the Director and Administrative Coordinator
Frank Culhane, Manager of Facilities and Security
Matthew Daugherty, IT Systems Administrator
Amy Dieringer, Visitor Services Representative
Zoe Donnell, Exhibitions and Publications Manager
Thomas Duke, Manager of Membership and Annual Giving
Tobin Eckholt, Development Services Manager
Cameron Fellows, Deputy Director and Director of Administration and Finance
Jon French, Visitor Services Representative
Alejandra Garceau, Store Clerk
Kara Hefley, Director of Development
Amy Hollister, Manager of Corporate and Foundation Relations
Rock Hushka, Director of Curatorial Administration and Curator of Contemporary and Northwest Art

Ellen Ito, Exhibition and Collection Assistant
Megan Jones, Visitor Services Manager
Laurel Jordan, Visitor Services Representative
Sloane King-Owen, Interim Museum Educator
Kris Knab, Cafe Staff
Boun Lameny, Security Officer
Bryce Macdonald, Security Officer
Alison Maurer, Curatorial Intern
Jeffrey Melton, Visitor Services Lead
Joshua Proehl, Interim Director of Education and Community Programs Manager
Linda Rabadi Fair, Associate Director of Development
Vitoria Ramos, Store Lead
Michelle Reynolds, Visitor Services Representative
Megan Ristine, Education and Volunteer Coordinator
Cyrus Smith, Museum Preparator
Jonathan Smith, Finance Manager
Jon Spencer, Chef and Cafe Manager
Pei Pei Sung, Graphic and Web Design Manager
Lisa Terry, Communications and PR Manager
Melissa Traver, Director of Marketing and Communications
Courtney Vowels, Public and Docent Programs Manager
Jessica Wilks, Registrar
Kristie Worthey, Associate Director of Museum Services